WOMEN IN AMERICA:
THE OPPRESSED MAJORITY

GOODYEAR SERIES IN AMERICAN SOCIETY
Jonathan H. Turner, Editor

INEQUALITY: PRIVILEGE & POVERTY IN AMERICA
Jonathan H. Turner and Charles E. Starnes

WOMEN IN AMERICA: THE OPPRESSED MAJORITY
Carol A. Whitehurst

URBAN AMERICA: PROBLEMS AND PROSPECTS
Edgar W. Butler

Forthcoming volumes will include perspectives on:

Crime in America
Social Stratification in America
Marriage and the Family in America

WOMEN IN AMERICA: THE OPPRESSED MAJORITY

Carol A. Whitehurst
The University of Iowa, Iowa City

Goodyear Publishing Company, Inc.   Santa Monica, California

Library of Congress Cataloging in Publication Data

Whitehurst, Carol A
   Women in America.

   (Goodyear series in American society)
   Includes index.
   1. Women—United States—Social conditions.
2. Women—United States—Economic conditions.
3. Feminism—United States. 4. Sex role.
I. Title.
HQ1426.W48   301.41'2'0973   76-16928
ISBN 0-87620-981-9
ISBN 0-87620-980-0 pbk.

Current printing (last digit):
10 9 8 7 6 5 4 3 2

ISBN: 0-87620-981-9 (C)
      0-87620-980-0 (P)

Y-9819-7 (C)
Y-9800-7 (P)

Manuscript and development editing: Sally Kostal
Cover design: Don McQuiston

Printed in the United States of America

To all the women and men of my Sex Roles classes at the University of California and the University of Iowa, who have contributed so much to my own learning, and to future students of Sex Roles, for whom this book is intended.

CONTENTS

PREFACE

This book is intended to be a general survey of sociological literature pertaining to women in American society and an analysis of woman's position in today's society. It is designed as an introductory work
and an overview for the individual who requires a summary of pertinent information regarding the institutional and cultural sources
circumscribing the role women play. Not all institutional arrangements
are explored, and a number of important issues, such as biological
differences between the sexes and female sexuality, are left to others
more versed in those areas. This book tends to deal more with white,
middle-class, relatively educated women than it does with minority
and blue-collar women. There are two reasons for this: first, because
the readership is likely to be relatively educated and probably middle-
class, the issues will be pertinent to them; and second, a great deal
more research literature exists on middle-class, educated, and professional women, and thus this book reflects the present state of knowledge in the field. New and important work is being done with regard to
minority and working-class women, but as yet data in this area is
scanty.

As I wrote this book it seemed to me important to attempt to review
as much literature as possible and to explore both sides of many argu-

ments; it seems that there are few (if any) black or white statements we can make about women in American society, and any conclusions we reach may be modified by subsequent evidence. Thus, it may appear often that I am unwilling to take a stand on many feminist issues. This is not for ideological reasons but for scholarly ones. On the other hand, I do have a point of view and an approach, and that approach is basically feminist. Thus, the conclusions, while based on a consideration of relevant research, are also always colored by my own ideological biases. It must be kept in mind that the conclusions are mine, and in no way reflect on the many people who contributed so much to this endeavor.

It isn't possible to acknowledge all of the people who have influenced the development of this book, for they are far too many and some are not even known to me by name. However, there are those people who played a direct role in the book's development, and others who gave me the support and encouragement I needed to continue with the long and sometimes tedious task of writing a book of this nature.

I especially want to thank Jonathan Turner, who suggested I write this book, edited it, and provided both helpful criticism and encouragement. Without his much appreciated help and suggestions the book could never have been written. Pat Golden, Mary Lindenstein Walshok, and Norma S. Wikler reviewed the manuscript and contributed many very valuable criticisms. Susan Steiner of Goodyear Publishing provided the push I sometimes needed to meet my deadlines.

To Lynn Munro Nollenberger, who contributed her time, patience, typing skills, and friendship, I am especially grateful. Special thanks are also in order for Martha Thompson and Maureen Farnan Steinberger who read and commented on portions of the manuscript, and who remained my friends even when it was difficult to do so. Lucile Whitehurst, my mother, has also been helpful both technically and emotionally, and to her I am thankful for much more than her contributions to this manuscript.

I would also like to acknowledge the contributions of colleagues Carl Couch, Lyle Shannon, and Mark Krain, who all suggested valuable ideas relevant to the book's framework. And finally, though certainly not least important, I wish to express thanks to the friends who were around me during the two years I was developing this book and who were invaluable aids in helping me to maintain my sanity. To Vicky Davison, Kathi Smith, Judy McKim, Karen Kerr, and Susan McQuin, I extend thanks for being patient friends and for helping me to increase my understanding of women in America.

1
REALITY IS SOCIALLY CONSTRUCTED

> "... sociology is justified by the belief
> that it is better to be conscious than uncon-
> scious, and that consciousness is a condition
> of freedom."
> —Peter L. Berger

The sophisticated realization on the part of feminists that the problems of women are not all from within, but are largely externally
imposed, has made a sociological analysis of women's situation relevant and appropriate. Much of the "condition of women" can be
explained by those things which are precisely sociological—institutions, roles, norms, values, and processes of socialization.

While social institutions possess an inertia of their own, they en-
dure because people come to think of them as the "way things should
be." People conform to and accept the subtle expectations of the world
around them.

Nowhere is the subtle power of social institutions more evident
than in the socialization of people into sex roles. The "feminine role"
and all the discriminatory forces inherent in this role are perpetuated
by the socialization process. By examining the socialization of women,
it becomes possible to understand why women are typically thrust
into inferior roles and why this situation has endured throughout
American history.

From *Invitation to Sociology,* copyright © 1963 by Peter L. Berger. Reprinted by permission of Doubleday & Company, Inc., and Penguin Books Ltd.

PATTERNS AND INSTITUTIONS

Members of a particular society and culture tend to take for granted the reality of everyday life, believing that their "knowledge" is somehow real, correct, and shared by everyone. But in fact, this knowledge is created by, and is the product of, a particular social context.[1] Actions which are repeated frequently become patterns, and since it is easier to follow patterns than constantly to make new decisions, these patterns come to be accepted as the way of doing things, as the reality of life, as institutions.

These institutions are legitimatized—explained and justified—to the new generation by the old through a process of socialization. Once institutions become fully legitimatized, they are no longer seen as simply human products which have, through habit, developed into accepted patterns for doing things, but are reified into an unalterable reality, based on something other than human production and social definition. Institutions may come to be seen as ordained by divine will, cosmic laws, or by nature. Therefore, their violation can be seen as the violation of the divinely constituted or naturally given order of the universe.[2]

The fact is that no institutional pattern is inevitable; it only seems that way because alternatives are infrequently presented. They are rarely presented because fewer alternatives give an illusion of order in our universe and of imposing order on our environment. Our definitions of appropriate behavior protect society from chaos and ourselves from anomie and psychic instability. Threats to the institutional order are not easily tolerated and are usually conquered or controlled in order to protect the structures of society.

Cultural life is infinitely more complex than this argument has suggested, and institutions are questioned. We have seen challenges to the social order by the so-called "hippie generation" and by the activists involved in civil rights and Vietnam protests. These groups have threatened the institutional order, and have influenced the ongoing structures of social life. However, general broad societal patterns persist despite protests and other threats.

Sociology has, as part of its task, to discover the hidden layers of social reality.[3] This involves analyzing the present institutions and the ideologies that maintain them. We can then effectively ask: What are the ideologies based on? What perpetuates these ideas? What needs do they fulfill? What functions do they serve? Until it is understood what vested interests and latent functions are involved in ongoing institutions and ideologies, it is meaningless to suggest strategies for change.

Institutions become part of human beings, establishing our roles, defining and limiting our existences. Deviance from established or prescribed roles is generally punished, or is allowed under only special circumstances and to a limited extent. On the whole, roles mean a set of expectations about conduct and attitudes which are pre-defined so that this conduct is taken for granted, often as if no other conduct were possible. The more the role is taken for granted, or the less it is questioned, the fewer will be the alternatives perceived and "the more predictable and controlled conduct will be."[4]

The situation of women in American society can profitably be evaluated in terms of the institutional arrangements into which women have been socialized. Originally, institutions may have been based on biological differences. That is, at one time, women's reproductive functions, the inability to control reproduction, women's smaller physical size, lesser muscular strength, and, possibly, lower average levels of aggression, may have limited women's ability to take part in the economic and political worlds. As the importance of biological differences has decreased, old patterns have persisted because people believe them to be not only correct but the only conceivable alternatives. Although it makes no sense any more to claim that the "natural sphere" of all women is the home, cultural patterns have made this claim appear natural and right. The fact that the "woman's role" has been accepted for so long attests to the power of socialization and the resulting internalization of societal norms and values.

Change Is Possible

While society defines us, it is also in turn defined by us, and thus can be changed.[5] If women choose to redefine their proper sphere in terms of what is proper for human beings, this redefinition should be possible. People must be convinced that this particular definition of social reality needs changing. Change is not a simple matter, particularly when few feel the need to change. It can be argued, however, that women are oppressed by the definitions and limits which institutions impose on them, and that freedom from these definitions would be less oppressive. It follows that the path to eliminating oppression would be to alter the institutional definition of the "proper activity" for women and men.

Some may, of course, disagree that freedom is desirable. After all, lack of freedom does narrow our choices and, when institutional arrangements are accepted, decision-making seems easier, and leads to greater stability in the social order. It is my belief, however, that knowledge is better than ignorance and that freedom is better than bondage. I believe that everyone should be made more aware of the possibilities and alternatives so that they have the opportunity to make these decisions for themselves.

WOMEN AS A MAJORITY

Although male births slightly outnumber female births,[6] at every other point in the life cycle, women constitute a majority of the citizens of the United States. While women comprise about 51 percent of all the people in the United States, by age 65 and over the male/female ratio is about 740/1000.[7] Yet, this majority group shows many of the characteristics of many minority groups. For, while women are a numerical majority with regard to enumeration by the census bureau, they are not a majority with power. In the world of work, politics, the media, and virtually all institutional spheres, save the family, women tend to be invisible.

It would not be accurate to say that women are really invisible in the world of work, since women now constitute close to 40 percent of the civilian labor force.[8] However, women are absent at those higher levels where decisions are being made, where large amounts of money are being distributed, and where high-level knowledge is being dispensed. Women basically make up that large body of workers known to the census bureau and researchers as "clerical and kindred" workers (34.5 percent of all women workers were in this category in 1974). Another 21.3 percent are found in the category of "service workers."[9]

It is also obvious that women are missing from another important sphere—the political arena. Again, women are the majority (about 53 percent) of registered voters,[10] but rarely hold elective offices and appointive governmental posts. Women, who make up a slight majority of constituents, not only find few women representatives, but almost none.

Table 1-1 Civilian labor force participation by women, 1950–74

	Numbers (in millions)	Percentage
1950	18.4	30%
1955	20.5	32%
1960	23.2	33%
1965	26.2	35%
1970	31.5	38%
1974	35.8	39%

Source: Table 2, U.S. Dept. of Labor, Bureau of Labor Statistics, *U.S. Working Women, A Chartbook,* 1975.

Table 1-2 Major occupation groups of employed women, 1959, 1964, 1969, and April 1974, women 16 years of age and over

Major occupational group	April 1974	1969	1964	1959
Total	100%	100%	100%	100%
Professional, technical	15.6	13.8	13.0	12.1
Managers, administrators	5.0	4.3	4.6	5.1
Sales workers	6.8	6.9	7.3	7.8
Clerical workers	34.5	34.3	31.2	29.9
Craft and kindred workers	1.4	1.2	1.0	1.0
Operatives	13.1	15.4	15.3	15.4
Nonfarm laborers	1.0	0.5	0.4	0.5
Service workers	21.3	21.6	23.9	23.5
Farm workers	1.4	2.0	3.3	4.8

Source: Table 36, p. 84, U.S. Dept. of Labor, Women's Bureau, *1975 Handbook on Women Workers.*

Women are beginning to be seen as newscasters, but largely are still missing from all sorts of media presentations, particularly when the presenter is, or seems to be, an authority figure or role model. A number of studies have shown how boys are overwhelmingly the main characters of stories in children's textbooks, and it has also been shown that men tend to be the authority figures in television commercials.[11] The vast majority of television programs have male stars,[12] and movies are presently being made almost exclusively about male main characters.[13] Everywhere males are presented as examples or as givers of advice, while females often are portrayed as less important figures.

OPPRESSION—DEFINITIONS AND FORMS

The dictionary defines *oppression* as a feeling of being weighed down, while to *oppress* means to keep down by the cruel or unjust use of power or authority. Thus, to oppress is to tyrannize or wield unjust power over, while being oppressed suggests an attitude of permanent hopelessness or psychological distress because of the burden of this tyranny.[14] Although originally used to describe the political stranglehold of a king or dictator subjugating his people, *oppression* is now often used to refer to the social or political subjugation of any group by another group. In this sense, it can easily be seen why *oppression* came to be adopted as one of the catchwords of the feminist movement. How better can one describe the rising sense of injustice that many women feel about being kept "in their place" by a group who is socially defined as being in power over them? The political implications of the word are clear—men are the oppressors, women the oppressed. According to this view, women are relegated to a secondary, subordinate position simply on the basis of their position in the power structure, since men hold the power in society and women do not.

Inner and Outer Oppression

Oppression has come to mean much more than being relegated to a secondary position. Oppression is used in describing the condition of a woman shut out from any activity, assigned "woman's work," kept from positions of leadership, denied access to positions or facilities, or forced into a certain kind of mold or stereotype. Oppression has come to be the word used to describe how women *feel* when they are told they either must do something or must not do something *simply because they are women*. The term oppression is not restricted to blatant or gross mistreatment, neglect, discrimination, or denial of jobs.

Oppression often means that all these things are being done very subtly—so subtly, in fact, that many women are taking part in their own oppression. Women have been denied jobs, for instance, because they weren't emotionally suited for the type of work involved, because they were intellectually inferior to men, and because they really didn't want to work anyhow. If women could be convinced that these things were true, that indeed their place was in the home, and that they would be much happier and more fulfilled people if they dedicated their lives to home and family, then obviously there would be no need to worry about denying them access to the world of work. It was only when women began to feel unfulfilled with the home sphere that they were in any position to feel slighted. And thus arose the notion of oppression—women are oppressed in the sense of being stereotyped, molded, and limited from the moment they are born.

Barriers and Limits to Achievement

To some women, oppression means barriers and limits on their ability to achieve. Some of these barriers are quota systems in admissions to graduate and professional schools, informal or formal norms in hiring women, and denial of equal access to the channels to achievement. Other women are oppressed by discrimination in wages, or lower pay for the same work, or even no pay for work defined as woman's duties. To still others, oppression is the lack of legal rights and equality under the law, including differential property rights, inheritance laws, and credit rations, as well as differential treatment under the law for certain kinds of behavior, particularly sexual behavior.

Many women feel their oppression not only in their unpaid labor, but in the fact that they almost always are assigned the menial tasks in the home, in offices, and in organizations. Because their work often seems trivial and demeaning, many women suffer oppression in the form of feelings of uselessness and meaninglessness. To some women, oppression seems specifically sexual. Because of their particular susceptibility to such assaults as rape and other physical violence, many women feel threatened and fearful. They are afraid to go out without an escort, afraid to be alone at night in their houses, afraid to drive long distances alone, afraid to travel alone or stay in hotels and motels alone, afraid to have a cocktail in a bar, unescorted. Some women are afraid to walk through or near a large group of men in a public place.

Others feel sexual oppression in the form of the new expectations of their sexuality, because of the widespread availability of the contraceptive pill. Because of the pill and the consequent freedom from the fear of pregnancy, some women feel they must be available for sex or be considered "hung-up." On the other hand, there is no evidence that the double standard has as yet vanished—women still are not expected to be sexual aggressors or to be insistent about their sexual needs or desires. Women with good healthy sex drives equal to those of many men tend to become defined, at best, as over-demanding and, at worst, as nymphomaniacs. And married women are less often allowed the freedom to "play around" than are married men.

Sex Objects
Women may also feel very much oppressed by being treated as sex objects. This does not mean that women do not want to be admired for their physical attributes, but that it is entirely objectionable *always* to be reacted to on this basis. How inappropriate it seems to a woman job applicant to be discussed in terms of her appearance when this would rarely be discussed in regard to a male applicant. And how degrading to be leered at rather than listened to when she is trying to present a point of view. In addition, physical attributes seem to be a double-edged sword, in that the woman who is very attractive often is discussed *only* in terms of her appearance, and sometimes even accused of using her sexuality to gain favor. The less attractive woman is also discussed in terms of her appearance, is criticized for "not doing something with herself," and sometimes is rejected for her homeliness. To be regarded as a sex object at some times by someone with whom one is intimately involved is certainly acceptable, but to be so regarded generally—by every man on the street, in the office, or any other place of business—is insulting and limits the possibilities of men and women relating to each other as equal human beings.

Beauty and Aging
Many women feel oppressed in another area of sexuality, the double standard of beauty and aging. Most women have, at some time, felt oppressed by the demand to be carefully made up, beautifully coiffed, and elaborately dressed. Many of us resent the time and the necessity for such artifice. The demand to be fashionable, to alter one's body or face, takes its toll on women who constantly feel the need to keep up this front and never to appear as their real, perhaps unacceptable, selves. The unhealthy overemphasis on youth, in our culture particularly, is oppressive to women. Men are thought to age gracefully, while a middle-aged woman is very often considered over-the-hill, not least of all by herself. The damaging effect this has on her self-concept is certainly another form of oppression.

Forced Dependency
Some women feel oppressed by their forced dependency. Because of their inability to survive on their own in a patriarchal world, they become possessions or shadows of the men to whom they are attached. In this position, a woman may feel herself to be no more than a servant to her master, as her fate is entirely up to him. This situation can lead to real anxiety when coupled with the fear of losing her attractiveness and ability to please the master. The knowledge that she

has no control over her own life can be extremely oppressive. The knowledge that one is party to one's own oppression can be equally oppressive.

Women can also be oppressed by the need to play games to survive. Many women learn to be deceitful, manipulative, and coy because they have learned that these are the only means the powerless can use to get their way. And yet, the necessity for these games, the necessity to play down one's talents or intelligence, to build up a man's ego at the expense of one's own, is psychically expensive and is totally repugnant to many women. It can be quite oppressive never to be yourself, never to be able to interact honestly and sincerely, and to feel triumph only when you are able to "put one over" on your opponent.

Women are also oppressed by the stereotyping which limits perceptions and expectations of what they can do and accomplish. In other words, if all women are expected to be wives and mothers, and to gain their essential fulfillment in that way, this expectation is severely oppressive to women who do not think that their only fulfillment lies in motherhood. Or if women are stereotyped as being flighty, emotional, sentimental, and unstable, then they obviously are unable to carry out the important work of the world. Even some of the less insidious stereotypes, which view women as supportive, helpful, and intuitive, work to limit their opportunities by channeling women only in directions which will take advantage of these "natural" talents.

Cute when Angry?

Finally, women are oppressed because they are not taken seriously. Women often are patronized, condescended to, and treated like children, even at times compared to and classified with children. Women are considered beings who have to be "handled," because they are not sufficiently rational to be dealt with as one would deal with a man. Women often are made the butt of jokes and are ridiculed, particularly for their efforts in behalf of women and women's rights. Their complaints and reports of mistreatment often are dismissed, treated lightly or even derisively. A woman often is not treated as if her opinions carry equal weight to those of a man, even if she has equal professional status. It is not uncommon that she is *literally* patted on the head when she becomes righteously indignant over an injustice. It is hard to imagine a male colleague being treated in such an insulting fashion, no matter how trivial his complaint. When male department members can refer contemptuously to "our token broad," or complain about the necessity for having a woman on every committee, or respond to a woman's complaint with "you're so cute when you get mad," it should be perfectly obvious that women are not being taken seriously, but are being considered on a level with children or idiots.

This form of oppression is particularly important because it is so basic to all other forms of oppression. Once women are no longer considered a joke and the idea of equality of the sexes is no longer something to be snickered about, they will have overcome many of the other forms of oppression. Only when women gain political leverage and thus are able to challenge men on their own territory will the movement for equality be taken seriously. As long as Women's Liberation can be defined as just one more whim, no real changes can be accomplished. To be taken seriously when one wants to be may be regarded as women's most basic goal.

Men, and sometimes other women, often have a way of translating a woman's description of her feelings of oppression into trivia. When women complain of frustration and boredom, men say they are harping about having too much leisure time, while claiming in the same breath that they wish they had more of it. Those who reject feminist demands often do so on the basis of peripheral issues, such as objections to the naming of hurricanes after women. They close their eyes to the importance of words and symbols, which shape reality, and the extent to which women might come to believe that men hold them in contempt by using such symbols. Or, some hold the issue of responsibility for birth control trivial and argue that contraception is overwhelmingly the responsibility of the woman, because a woman's birth control pill was easier to develop and because women, who have more to lose, *should* be responsible for preventing pregnancy. Again, this argument underscores the fact that many men are *not* equally willing to assume responsibility for an act which is equally theirs, while at the same time conveniently ignoring the suffering or, at the very least, the unpleasant and annoying side effects of contraceptive devices and other birth control measures.

A Pedestal Is a Precarious Place
Some people find it strange that women can feel oppressed by being placed on a pedestal. But most people do not want to be unrealistically idealized and worshipped at the expense of their equality and individuality. "Worship" is a poor substitute for genuine regard and respect, especially when meted out on the condition that one must stay in that very precarious, circumscribed place. But, it is not so much being put on a pedestal which is oppressive—it is using this as an excuse for denying women equality. A pedestal is not necessarily a pleasant, and certainly not an easy, place to be. Persons who live on pedestals have a very precarious existence and are constantly in danger of falling off. It is much easier, and really more acceptable to most people, to be viewed not from above, as with contempt, and not from below,

as with worship, but eye-to-eye, with understanding and respect for their opinions and ways of coping.

Many tend to cloud the issue by asking, as if in disbelief, whether a woman really gets offended when a man opens a door for her, implying that this is trivial and human beings have far more important issues to worry about. Again, opening doors is only symbolic, for feminists do want to forego this treatment if it means that they will continue to be treated nonseriously, as sex-objects, discriminated against, stereotyped, and denied power. On the other hand, most sincere people of both sexes simply answer that they hold doors open for others of either sex and are happy to have others open doors for them, depending on convenience and the desire to show another person a simple courtesy.

No feminist is asking that she be treated impolitely. She is simply asking that everyone be treated politely, without regard to sex, and that she is not thrown a bone in the form of small courtesies while basic human rights of equality of opportunity are being denied.

American Women Pampered?

Some argue that American women are not oppressed—that they are the most pampered, leisured, privileged class anywhere. While for a certain limited segment of upper-middle-class or upper-class non-working married women (a relatively small proportion of adult women[15]) this may seem to be true, lack of oppression cannot be equated simply with leisure time and relative affluence. A person who is basically parasitic, nonproductive, and inessential also may be extremely bored, frustrated, fatigued, and depressed. These are symptoms of a kind of oppression—an oppression which defines one's status as an object of consumption and an appropriate adjunct to one's husband.

CONCLUSION

Oppression is a term which means a great many things to different people. For our purposes, oppression will be taken to mean being systematically denied access to power and being limited in developing one's potential fully in every area of life. Accordingly, oppression is not a term which can be applied to white, middle-class males, since they, as a group, are not being systematically denied access to power. However, to the extent that men also are limited by stereotypes and prejudices in developing their potential fully, they are also oppressed. While this situation is recognized, and is certainly held to be important, it is not my purpose to present a case for the oppression of men. Rather, the purpose is to deal with the question of why women have not achieved on a level equal to that of men. The answer to this question lies not in the inherent inferiority or lack of ambition in women, but in the oppressive structures of American society.

Four major institutional structures have oppressed and limited the achievement and psychological fulfillment of women. The four institutions to be discussed are the family; the educational institutions; the economic or occupational institutions; and the political institutions. It will be shown further how cultural values have served to perpetuate women's secondary, subordinate status in contemporary American society.

NOTES

1. The framework for this entire section is from Peter L. Berger and Thomas Luckmann, *The Social Construction of Reality* (Garden City, N.Y.: Doubleday Anchor Books, 1967).

2. Ibid., p. 99.

3. Peter L. Berger, *Invitation to Sociology: A Humanistic Perspective* (Garden City, N.Y.: Anchor Books, 1963), p. 21.

4. Berger and Luckmann, op. cit., p. 62.

5. Berger, op. cit., p. 129.

6. The actual male/female ratio in 1970 was 1050/1000. Abbott L. Ferris, *Indicators of Trends in the Status of American Women* (New York: Russell Sage Foundation, Harper and Row, 1973).

7. Ibid., p. 14.

8. Ibid., p. 379, gives 37.3% in 1969.

9. Ibid., pp. 374–375.

10. U.S. Bureau of the Census, *Current Population Reports*, no. 244 (Washington, D.C.: Govt. Printing Office, December 1972).

11. Janet Saltzman Chafetz, *Masculine/Feminine or Human? An Overview of the Sociology of Sex Roles* (Itasca, Ill.: F. E. Peacock, 1974), p. 52; also Lucy Komisar, "The Image of Woman in Advertising," in *Woman in Sexist Society*, ed. Vivian Gornick and Barbara Moran (New York: Basic Books, 1971), pp. 304–317.

12. Chafetz, op. cit., p. 52; David Denby, "Men Without Women, Women Without Men," *Harper's* 247 (September 1973); Maureen Orth, "How to Succeed: Fail, Lose, Die," *Newsweek* 4 (March 1974); Molly Haskell, *From Reverence to Rape* (New York: Harper and Row, 1973).

13. Chafetz, op. cit., p. 53.

14. Webster's *New Collegiate Dictionary*, ed., s.v., "oppression."

15. Ferris, op. cit.

ADDITIONAL REFERENCES

1. Friedan, Betty. *The Feminine Mystique*. New York: Dell, 1963.

2. Hacker, Helen Mayer. "Woman as a Minority Group." *Social Forces* 30, October 1957, pp. 60–69.

3. Janeway, Elizabeth. *Man's World, Woman's Place*. New York: Delta, 1971, p. 176.

4. Women on Words and Images. *Dick and Jane as Victims*. p. 6.

2
MARRIAGE, FOR BETTER OR FOR WORSE?

> *"The tragedy of marriage is not that it fails to assure women the promised happiness — there is no such thing as assurance in regard to happiness — but that it mutilates her; it dooms her to repetition and routine."*
> —*Simone de Beauvoir*

Most women and men in America marry and have families. Although many marry because they want to be together, most people marry for different, largely unconscious reasons. Women, denied full access to the more satisfying and/or remunerative careers, find the economic security of marriage the logical choice. Men, having little skill and less interest in household management and child rearing, find that marriage relieves them of domestic responsibilities while supplying them with a family life. As an added bonus, both sexes find that they are considered "complete" adults once they enter into the statuses of spouse and parent.

SEXUAL DIVISION OF LABOR
In recent years, many family writers and researchers have come to the same conclusion regarding women's oppression. One of the feminist movement's earliest theorists and activists and the author of the widely read *Dialectic of Sex*, Shulamith Firestone, says, "the heart of woman's oppression is her childbearing and childrearing roles."[1]

From Simone de Beauvoir, *The Second Sex*, ed. and trans. H. M. Parshley (New York: Alfred A. Knopf, Inc., 1970), p. 451.

According to this view of woman's bondage to her biology, and the patterns (dependency and love and duty to family) which grow out of the biological fact of procreation, it is not marriage or family per se which is the source of oppression, but the sexual division of labor. This division is institutionalized in the family.

Anthropologists trace the origin of the sexual division of labor to the fact that women in many primitive societies, having borne the children, stayed home in order to nurse and care for them. In a hunting and gathering society, they usually performed the less mobile occupations. Being a gatherer and tending a household was not inherently inferior to being a hunter, as the division of labor was built on partnership and the total interdependence of women and men. But women's roles in childbearing, childrearing, household management, and sedentary tasks near the home, and the degree of their importance as food gatherers, meant that they became the "second sex" in hunting societies. Power differentials developed as men came to possess weapons and other means of physical power. More and more, men came to do the "important" work of the world and to acquire power over their immediate families. Kathleen Gough argues that the division of labor became institutionalized with the rise of the state and class society. Women became the property of their husbands, and often possessed no legal rights of their own. Shulamith Firestone thinks that "nature produced the fundamental inequality, which was later consolidated or institutionalized in the interests of men."[2] What was originally a convenient and functional pattern became institutionalized even though the sexual division of labor became less critical for social survival.

Other sociologists, including Juliet Mitchell, have argued that the origin of the oppression of women lies in the demand for private property and the development of a patriarchal system in which a man had to have exclusive sexual rights to his wife to ensure the legitimacy of his offspring. Mitchell does not hold a simplistic economic view of woman's oppression, but finds woman's status determined in four key structures of society: production, reproduction, sexuality, and socialization of children. According to Mitchell, "The causal chain then goes: maternity, family, absence from production and public life, sexual inequality."[3]

Otherness
Simone de Beauvoir's discussion of the "Otherness" of women grows out of her analysis of both the economic and the reproductive aspects of women's subordinate position. According to this idea of Otherness, men represent the standard, the norm, the ideal. Thus, woman is always the Other, somehow mysterious and unintelligible and inferior. Women are given their own place and world—that of the home and family. But this place becomes a woman's natural destiny,

the stage for her achievements and her prison. It is as if providing her with her own place is meant to compensate for her exclusion from the world of production and power.[4]

Elizabeth Janeway argues that although women had fewer legal and political rights a century or two ago, their roles were far less restricted. In the past, when many women were connected with farms and large families, they had a great number of functions, many of which were quite important. Women not only were responsible for managing children and household (which meant managing a number of servants who had to be taught skills and to do chores), but often women were involved in economically valuable work. Many produced salable merchandise in the form of cloth, animals, eggs, dairy products, fruits, and vegetables. Producing and selling such items meant that women might have a certain amount of economic independence, as well as a sense of pride in their productive abilities. They also might have achieved a sense of identity from knowing they did something well and receiving recognition from the objective, outside world. Thus, women used their energies and talents fully and were active useful members of the community. In that sense, women were less restricted than many of today's housewives who are confined to the home in less meaningful and less satisfying roles.

Complementary Roles
Family theory of the 1950s and much of the 1960s was based on the notion of interdependent roles in which one member of the marital pair played the instrumental or task role, the other the socioemotional or expressive role. In Talcott Parsons' development of this theory, the roles were held to be clearly not "equal" but "equally important." That is to say, husbands tended to provide instrumental functions for the family, in terms of breadwinning, status-determination, decision-making, and authority. Wives provided the socioemotional or expressive functions as homemakers, providing emotional support for the task leader and relieving the provider of housekeeping and child care responsibilities. This division of labor was posited to be necessary for the functioning of the existing economic system. Because of the interdependence of its members, the family was believed to be becoming an ever stronger unit. The asymmetrical relationship which developed between husband and wife was seen as functional in that it eliminated the competition for status which might be disruptive to the solidarity of the marriage.[5]

Parsons admitted this division of functions also could be a source of strain for women, who were not allowed to compete on an equal basis with men. He felt that many women succumbed to their conflicts through neurotic illness or compulsive domesticity. To Parsons, then, it was functional for society to define half the population as the homemakers and childrearers, and the other half as the breadwinners, achievers, policy-makers, and leaders, despite individual strains. Marital roles were therefore complementary, or "separate but equal."

The "Colleague Family"

In another influential book written about the same time as Parsons', Daniel Miller and Guy Swanson introduced the idea of the "colleague family," in which each partner provides skills and interests that the other may lack. Each could defer to the other's judgments on the grounds of differing competence, thus preserving the equality of the relationship.[6] This description of an ideal family form sounds appealing until one considers that the things the housewife tends to know about and excel at are considered trivial, and all the real power and decision-making ability lies in the hands of the person supporting the family. "Separate but equal" cannot be equal in fact if occupational status is *the* measure of status in a society, and if providing support to the family gives the supporter the *right* to power.

Despite the trend toward equalizing legal obligations and rights in the family, there is no research evidence that equalitarianism in actual relationships between wife and husband is increasing. The word "equal" implies interchangeable units, but nowhere in American society are the rights and duties of wives and husbands totally interchangeable.[7]

Other family researchers are in agreement with this recent analysis of changing roles. John Scanzoni has reported that although there has been a change over time from women as property to women as complements, only a minute percentage of wives are in equal partnership roles.[8] Scanzoni has concluded that husbands have more power because they have more resources, and the key to equality is access to resources which will enable women to bargain more effectively. (This notion is supported by research which has shown that the working wife has more authority than her nonworking counterpart.)[9] Other researchers also have noted the lack of equality in marital relationships; for instance, Robert Blood and P. M. Wolfe found clear evidence of the husband's greater power in eight different areas of family decision-making.[10]

MYTHS

Various myths about the family exist which tend to orient our thinking in particular directions. The family may not be the source of all oppression of women, but, especially in its more traditional forms, it does perpetuate unequal patterns for women and men.

Equalitarian Myth

A great deal of lip service has been paid to the idea of equal roles for women. This has tended to be more on ideological and verbal levels than on behavioral levels, and families today are probably no more "equalitarian" (in the sense of interchangeability of roles) than they have been in the past. Although the husbands of working wives participate more in home life (especially child care) than do the husbands of nonworking wives, the participation does not reach the level of equality, or full sharing of all tasks.[11] The companionate form of marriage has been the trend, and it implies a breakdown of sexual polarity and a greater overlapping of sexual spheres. The expansion of women's economic roles has brought about a wider distribution of domestic responsibilities.[12] However, an increase in the number of husbands washing dishes or doing the grocery shopping does not represent true equality for women, and it has not created a situation for women in which they can "reach the top" as easily as men.

One family researcher, Ira Reiss, believes that full equality in the family is not possible as long as family and occupational roles differ by sex. Since men are not willing to assume household roles, he argues, women must work to develop day care centers so that they may contribute to family support. The answer to greater equality seems to be in the economic arrangement—a woman's contribution to the decision-making process correlates directly with her value as measured by the outside world. Wives who work outside the home and contribute to family income have more authority and bargaining power in the family. The obvious implication is that true equality of marital roles is not possible unless both members of the marital pair are contributing to its economic support.

The best evidence available shows that (1) if equality is what is wanted, economic responsibility must be shared; and (2) as long as a woman is defined as a childrearer whose first responsibility is to her family, equality is not possible. The goal may not be equality of roles, but it is important to recognize that the equalitarian model of the family is a myth which exists only under extraordinary circumstances.

Myth of Family Breakdown

Another important myth about the contemporary family is that marital breakups are reaching crisis proportions and that the family may be coming to an end. Divorce rates have been increasing, and continue to increase, but modern marriage is neither collapsing nor passé. The trend is toward a steadily increasing divorce rate, but the refined rate now shows the proportion of divorces per year to be approaching 2 percent of the population base of marriageable women. While this still does not necessarily represent an *alarming* increase over previous years, the census bureau reports that the nation's divorce rate in the last four years increased as much as it had in the previous ten years. There has also been an increase in the proportion of single young persons establishing their own households.[13]

Remarriage rates are extremely high, and about 90 percent of all people can be expected to marry at some time. Rather than finding

Table 2-1 Divorces in the United States, per year, per 1,000 population and refined rate,[a] 1940–74.

	1940	1950	1955	1960	1965	1970	1971	1972	1973	1974
Per 1,000	2.0	2.6	2.3	2.2	2.5	3.5	3.7	4.0	4.4	4.6
Refined	8.8	10.3	9.3	9.2	10.6	14.9	15.9	16.9	NA	NA

Source: Table 94, "Marriages and Divorces: 1940 to 1974," *Statistical Abstract of the U.S.*, U.S. Dept. of Commerce, 1975.

[a]Number of divorces per year in a cohort of 1,000 married women age 15 and over.

that the family is disappearing or even becoming unpopular, a national survey of adults in 1973 showed that support for the family was quite strong. Eighty percent of the adult respondents said that a happy family life was the most important of four possible goals (including also personal development, career, and money). Over 75 percent of the sample agreed that "the traditional family is important to American society and should be preserved." On the other hand, expectations about the form of the family are undergoing change, as 75 percent agreed that it was perfectly all right for married couples to choose not to have children. Also, a majority felt young couples should delay having children until they had had a few years alone together. Even still, almost half agreed with the statement that "woman's place is in the home," and 44 percent supported a division of sex roles by agreeing with the following statement: "Traditionally, men in our society have had certain responsibilities and women have had others. This is the way it should be."[14]

The results of the survey indicate that about half of the adult population holds rather traditional attitudes toward women being in the home, but far more seem to view the family as an important, valuable institution. The high remarriage rates indicate that, far from rejecting marriage, they are actually supporting the institution and reaffirming the value of the personal commitment by taking on another when the first fails to meet their needs. The fact that individuals will go to these lengths to protect and to continue this tie indicates its strength and importance. Therefore, despite the dire predictions and widespread cynicism about marriage and the family, it does not appear that either institution will disappear in the near future.

Marriage and Work Myths

Another myth (or set of myths) about marriage and the family is that women's working outside the home is detrimental to marital happiness and to children. This myth forms the backbone of the resistance to women's liberation, to the movement of women out of the home and into the work world.

A woman's freedom to choose among alternative life styles is an important predictor of happiness in marriage. Both partners in marriage seem to be happier if the wife participates in the labor force from choice rather than out of economic necessity. A woman's choice of the labor market over the home strains the marriage only when there are preschool children in the family. Having a *choice* seems to be the crux for happiness, as the families of women who work because they want to are distinctly better off than the families of women who work because they have to. Also, if women choose to work outside the home, they are happier than if they prefer to work but must stay at home.[15]

Maternal employment produces a more symmetrical family structure with greater equality between husbands and wives,[16] and it seems that with the wife's greater power and role in decision making there will be a more equalitarian, companionate relationship. Thus, marriages of career women may well be happier and more fulfilling than those of housewives.[17] Present studies show that almost all young women indicate that their future plans include both family and career. This can mean added benefits, but it can contribute to additional strain as well.

Effect on children. The debate over how mothers' careers influence children is much more controversial and somewhat less clear. Eleanor Maccoby concluded from her research that a child did have a need for one consistent person as nurturer.[18] Kibbutz children, without one consistent nurturing person, seemed to suffer from "maternal" deprivation and insufficient nurturance which led to psychological withdrawal and hostility.[19] It has been found that if a mother likes her work, it has good effects on her children[20] and that mothers who prefer to work but who, out of a sense of "duty," do not work report the most problems in child rearing.[21] Harbeson, reporting on Bowlby's careful WHO monograph, concluded: the *quality* of the parental care which the child receives in his earliest years is of vital importance for his future mental health.[22] There is no unequivocal evidence that outside employment of mothers affects children favorably or unfavorably. On the basis of all the conflicting data, no valid generalization is possible. It is not so much the quantity of mothering, or the time spent, but the quality of interaction between parent and child, which refers to the warmth, affection, and care going into the relationship. No study has shown the necessity that the nurturer be the child's mother, or even a woman, although much of the research is based on the assumption that the mother is the "natural" childrearer and that it is her absence which may have deleterious effects.

Rochelle Wortis, in a careful review of the child-care literature, questioned the primacy of the mother-child bond. She also questioned the assumptions that the attachment of the child was to its mother, that there was an instinct for motherhood, and that the best environment for rearing a child was the home. She concluded that social scientists and clinicians have accepted as necessary and inevitable, practices that are culturally determined. She felt they generally seemed unable to explore alternatives because of their biased conception of what should be studied and their satisfaction with the status quo.[23]

It seems clear enough that very young children may suffer from deprivation of affection and nurturing, but there is no evidence to support the view that *maternal* deprivation is the culprit. Any consistent warm adult might do as well as the child's mother. Again, the concept of what seems right and natural (and, in fact, the only way to do things) seems nothing more than a social construction. However, this "reality" which we have constructed has shaped and continues to shape the lives of most women and men in our society.

Childrearing and the Motherhood Mystique

Jessie Bernard has said, "In our country today, motherhood takes precedence over wifehood."[24] A long-time trend toward greater emphasis on the maternal role is only beginning to be challenged and full-time devotion to motherhood is no longer a taken-for-granted way for women to pursue happiness. In fact, today there is a critical attitude toward over-maternity. Nevertheless, "motherhood as a value is inculcated into girls from such an early age that alternatives are hardly given serious attention."[25]

Simone de Beauvoir discusses the Cult of Maternity, which she describes as a myth concerning the saintliness and devotion of mothers to their children. She states that maternity is not enough in all cases to crown a woman's life—there are many mothers who are embittered, unhappy, and unsatisfied. There is nothing "natural" or instinctual about mother love.[26] However, "from infancy woman is told over and over that she is made for childbearing, and the splendors of maternity are forever being sung to her. The drawbacks of her situation . . . are all justified by this marvelous privilege she has of bringing children into the world."[27] The mystique of the glories of childbirth, the grandeur of "natural" female creativity, and the glories and creativity of childrearing have contributed to women's oppression by keeping her in this single defined sphere. "The Freudian mythos was invoked to justify a repeated affirmation of the enormous importance of woman's natural role as mother. . . . Mothers . . . do not have to look for creative careers because the very nature of their noblest and most significant task is creation."[28] Thus, we have the myth that if one is able to create another human being, all other creativity pales in comparison, and is entirely unnecessary. Men, who cannot create in this way, must invent, compose, paint, or produce in some other way to compensate.

The Myth that Marriage Fills Women's Lives

One of the major reasons that the family seems to be undergoing such radical change is that various social and technological developments have drastically altered the family life cycle. The post-World War II increase in the employment of married women has been accompanied by a decline in the birthrate, the earlier completion of childbearing, and the decreasing work week.[29] The decline in the birthrate has been steady since the late 1800s, when it was 37 births per 1000 population. By the 1930s it had dropped to about 18 per 1000, increasing somewhat again in the 1950s to about 23–25 per 1000 and declining again more recently to the 15 per 1000 in 1974.[30] The declining birthrate has meant smaller families and a shortening of the period in which the family is producing children. The total phase has decreased, so that children are more closely spaced. Mothers have their children early, closely spaced, and few in number, so that the mother is younger now when the last child leaves the home. While in 1890 the "empty-nest" mother was about 55–56, in 1960 she was 47. Added to this, today's woman has a much longer life expectancy and can be expected to live about 25 years after her last child has gone. In contrast, a woman's life expectancy in 1900 was only 48.7 years.

All of the above data on the life cycle of the family point to the conclusion that neither childbearing nor childrearing can take up all of an adult woman's life. Women also generally outlive their husbands by a few years, leaving them without even a *marital* role late in life. A certain proportion of women never marry (about 10 percent), another group are divorced or separated, and another widowed, which again destroys the myth of marriage "filling" women's lives. Though the majority of women have a spouse and children in the home, it is clear from the description of the life cycle that they will be "out of a job" relatively early in life when their children leave the home. These women run the risk of suffering from the "empty-nest syndrome" of depression and neuroticism because of their loss of role. This period can be especially difficult if the woman has no other pursuits except those of providing for her family. It is even more difficult if her financial position is insecure and she has no means of supporting herself should she find herself without a spouse.

Thus, the myth that marriage and family are sufficient goals for any woman is belied by the timing of the family life cycle. This cycle limits childbearing to a very short period in a woman's twenties, and childrearing to a maximum of about twenty-five years, after which the woman is largely functionless and often depressed. Whether or not the family itself is oppressive, the fact is that preparing for nothing but future family roles cannot be considered the wisest course in light of the current trends in life cycle, life expectancy, and marital stability.

EFFECTS OF MARRIAGE/FAMILY ON WOMEN

Housekeeping Functions

While marriage is good for men in terms of mental health, suicide rates, and longevity, marriage seems to be bad for women in terms of mental health and commission of crimes. Married women, in numerous studies of adjustment and happiness, are more depressed and anxious than married men, while married men are happier than unmarried men. Married men are less likely to commit suicide than unmarried men, while married women are more likely to commit suicide than unmarried women. Married women tend to have higher utilization rates of mental facilities than do married men, although there are exceptions to this finding. In general, married women fare poorly compared to both married men and unmarried women.

Table 2-2 Institutional population by sex in four psychiatric facilities for patients age 18–64, 1968

	General hospitals	State and county	Outpatient	Private
Men	119,443 (40%)	121,903 (54%)	70,470 (38%)	26,673 (39%)
Women	177,103 (60%)	105,195 (46%)	113,392 (62%)	40,965 (61%)

Source: NIMH, "Patients in Mental Health Facilities," U.S. Dept. of HEW, Public Health Service, Health Services and Mental Health Administration, 1969.

While men are expanded by taking on the role of husband, a woman "dwindles" into being a wife. This involves a redefinition of the self and a reshaping of personality. Being relegated to the role of housewife is worse for her than marriage *per se*, as a large part of the "deforming" of the woman's mind to shape her for happiness in marriage is accounted for by the nature of the tasks she performs. Although most young women before marriage indicate little or no positive interest in the domestic arts, they find that this becomes their major function. Housework is menial labor, low status, unpaid, never-ending, and dead-end in the sense that there is no way to be promoted to a higher level. This may have a deteriorating effect on a woman's mind, and the isolation which comes from being imprisoned in a nuclear household can lead to erratic judgments, a sense of powerlessness, and susceptibility to psychosis.[31]

Women in limited spheres seem to become small minded, petty; they pursue trifles, lack concentration, and are given to daydreaming and mindwandering, brooding, fatigue, and psychosomatic symptoms. ". . . The functions women perform affect their personalities, character, and mentality: they become creatures of their sphere."[32]

Although the nature of dirty, never-ending and dead-end work is itself unsatisfying, it is made worse by the fact that no one is willing to share the tasks. Housework has been described as a political issue because the reason housework is defined as women's work is that men will not lower themselves to do it.[33] A woman cannot help but know that her work is considered trivial, unimportant, and demeaning, and she may lack a source of self-esteem. This work is so narrow that women have to beware of becoming narrow themselves, with few outside interests and little knowledge of important events.

> *What does our oppression within the family do to us women? It produces a tendency to small mindedness, petty jealousy, irrational emotionality, and random violence, dependency, competitive selfishness and possessiveness, passivity, a lack of vision and conservatism. . . . You cannot inhabit a small and backward world without it doing something to you.*[34]

A number of "feminine" traits frustration can engender are self-pity, timidity, silliness, and self-consciousness. The only antidote to these feelings, to the grave self doubts, the need to please, and the fear of not being wanted (which most women feel at some time) is a sense of one's own value.[35]

The family is maintained at the expense of women. Because there is no recognition of the value of their labor, women are left with no sense of value as a group at all. The work is not valued because no goals are being pursued, the actual nature of the work is, in a sense, invisible and it is never done. This leaves one with no sense of satisfaction or accomplishment. Beliefs that female traits include noncompetition, delicacy, incompetence, softness, masochism, the capacity for boring work, hysteria, emotionalism, and sentimentality serve a useful purpose in keeping women in their place, preserving free female labor and service.[36]

Simone de Beauvoir also has discussed how in seeking to find justification in housework and homemaking, women find no escape from their secondary status and little affirmation of their individuality. The attempt dooms the individual woman to the unessential and makes her useful only through her help to others.[37]

In addition to this psychological narrowing and trivialization from being confined to housework, is the accompanying problem that women who are confined to the home are also both financially and psychologically dependent on the breadwinner.

Stroking Functions
A related issue is the fact that women are expected to perform the "stroking" or supportive functions in a marriage. Although few would agree that the stroking function ought to be abandoned, many question the fact that this role is allocated to women. In other words, although the family or marital relationship is often seen as an outlet for

emotional tension, this outlet often works in only one direction. Studies of blue-collar marriages, for example, have shown that there is no reciprocation of support or tension-releasing functions, indicating that women absorb all the tensions while men refuse to do the same.[38] This allocation of roles reflects the attitude that it is a woman's responsibility to "keep him happy." Research shows both that women tend to make greater adjustments in marriage[39] and that men are on the whole much happier with marriage than are women.[40] Women have always been defined as the sacrificers, the ones to adjust and mold themselves to their families' needs. While it may not necessarily lead to poorer mental health, there is evidence that these requirements have a negative psychological effect on women.[41]

Blue-Collar/White-Collar

Problems for blue-collar wives and middle-class wives are not always the same, as middle-class women tend to suffer from the "problem that has no name,"[43] or from feelings of frustration, lack of fulfillment, and inability to put to use their education and skills.

Psychologist Phyllis Chesler has argued that the marital relationship, to the extent that it emphasizes the acceptance of the "feminine role," can result in a "slave psychology" and chronic fatigue states in married women. Citing national statistics on the greater numbers of women in mental health facilities and in therapy, Chesler points out how the acceptance of the dependent, even helpless, role creates mental problems (especially depression) as well as ensures that they will be more likely to passively accept hospitalization. Analyzing the higher rates of mental illness in women, Gove and Tudor found that it was specifically *married* women who were more likely to be mentally ill than married men. Gove explained this on the basis of greater role conflict for married women.[42]

Jessie Bernard says there are greater mental health hazards in marriage to women than to men, and propounds a "shock theory of marriage" in which she argues that marriage is more of a shock to women than to men, because they are expected to dwindle into a more submissive and conservative role, to make greater adjustments (although she feels women's disenchantment with the strengths, etc. of their husbands are much more profound than his with hers), to feel neutered sexually as she becomes older and is identified as a mother and a housewife, and because she is subjected to the unending trivia and meaninglessness of housework. (See Table 2-3.) They also may be forced into glamor and hostess roles which may or may not be compatible with their wishes, temperaments, and other roles. Blue-collar wives do not necessarily share these problems, but the high point in their lives may have been catching a man and marrying. After that, there may be few sources of gratification, and once her youth is gone,

Table 2-3 Proportion (%) of impaired respondents in midtown Manhattan mental health survey for married respondents

Age	Men	Women
20–29	11.7	13.4
30–39	19.6	22.1
40–49	19.0	18.1
50–59	25.7	30.6

Source: Leo Srole et al. *Mental Health in the Metropolis: The Midtown Manhattan Study*, New York: McGraw-Hill, 1972, pp. 177–178.

there may be few sources of self-esteem for the blue-collar wife.

Sociologist Mirra Komarovsky's important and well-known study of blue-collar families, actually carried out in the late 1950s, seems to be the primary source of our knowledge of sex role behavior in the working class. At that time Komarovsky found a situation in which women and men of her blue-collar community lived in totally different psychological worlds. While men had their world of work and men's activities, liking to talk shop and use vulgarity, women had their home worlds, liking to discuss children and family events. Komarvosky found the things men and women talked about were entirely different, and each had their own interests, attitudes, and concerns, which rarely overlapped those of the opposite sex. Perhaps most important of all, although both sexes suffered from what Komarovsky called a "trained incapacity to communicate" because of the relative meagerness of their joint social life, men had even greater difficulties with communication because of their own rigid norms of masculinity. These norms held that it was appropriate for men to suppress their emotions, to deny the possibility of hurt or weakness, and to inhibit self-disclosure about anything which might make him appear to be less of a man. Komarovsky has documented the lack of communication and other rewarding aspects of the blue-collar wife's marital relationship. Working-class families are perhaps more bound than middle-class by rigid concepts of masculinity. While working-class women may not have the career and fulfillment problems of middle-class wives, they often have problems of too little money and meaningless routine work.[44] They also lack work satisfaction and are likely to turn to their families, but this may result in even greater dissatisfaction and resultant depression because of the relatively unrewarding marital relationship. In blue-collar marriages, the two different worlds the sexes inhabit are quite separate, with only minimal and superficial overlap.[45]

Two major concerns of working-class, middle-aged women. Susan Jacoby studied a consciousness-raising group of working-class middle-aged women. While many of the concerns of the Women's Liberation Movement may not have seemed relevant to the women in this group, two major concerns emerged from the group which apply to women everywhere. One concern was with the fact that they were *no longer viewed as sexually interesting* despite the fact that they had not themselves renounced an interest in sex or in feeling attractive. (This issue will be discussed in the chapter on psychological oppression.) The second concern was that *they felt themselves to be "out of a job" in terms of care of a family.* To this group, even though educational achievement was not high, having an occupation became a priority. Even mundane jobs could be opportunities to many women with no training, experience, or high aspirations. These women were not rebelling against the oppression of the family, which had been fulfilling in many senses, but they were realistically attempting to fill the gap when the mothering role no longer existed.[46]

BARRIERS TO ACHIEVEMENT

It is commonly observed that homemaking and child care responsibilities assigned to women add to the difficulties of pursuing a career, especially in terms of time and energy and role conflicts. Families limit women by putting a ceiling on the energy and emotion any woman feels she can afford to invest in her job.[47] A woman is expected to see that her household runs properly and that her children are looked after. If she is unable to manage her side of the marriage contract, she should not work: "as the Women's Liberation Movement sees very clearly, this obligation is probably the largest barrier to sex equality today, for by accepting it, women accept a special place and a special role."[48]

Married women less often than men or unmarried women rise to the tops of their professions. Society demands that women's duties as mothers override their other role obligations, and these family obligations interfere with handling the demands of a career. In addition to the demands on her time, the duties and obligations of a wife and mother are not compatible with those of a worker or a career woman. Rather than reinforcing and complementing a work role as they do in the case of men, marriage and family roles are seen as conflicting with women's work roles. If a woman adds the strains of her outside occupation, her home role as tension manager will be decreased, and the family will suffer. There are a number of negative pressures on wives who work: husbands may feel the loss of the supporter, and they may feel threatened or deprived. Children may not see any advantage to their mother having a career. Others may feel she is neglecting the importance of the mother-child relationship, and society still defines childhood crises as the province of the mother.

Running a house or family is a time-consuming task, made more so by the emphasis placed on the quality of child-care and home life, cooking, decorating, sanitation, and interaction with children. Every person who wants to have a career or produce as a professional needs a "wife" to do all the time-consuming things, as well as to provide the emotional support to free them for their creativity or productivity. Research on dual-career families tends to support the idea that families act as brakes on women's drive toward achievement in careers. For many women, the attempt to have a full-fledged career while raising a family creates problems of conflict and strain, although many wives learn to accommodate to the conflicts, and others develop new patterns. Sociologist Margaret Poloma found that there was little role conflict in her study of women actively engaged in law, medicine, or college teaching. This was because women worked in careers, but did not *have* careers in the same sense as men. They paced their work and professional progress, and conflicts were resolved in favor of home role demands. Poloma concluded that the professional employed wife and mother created a psychologically comfortable position for herself by defining the situation as one of work with emphasis on family.[49]

In a later study, Margaret Poloma and Neal Garland referred to this pattern in which women are socialized to tolerate or accept marriage and family as their primary goal as a "tolerance of domestication." This "tolerance" means that women do not set their sights very high, and usually do not train for a specific field, or if they do, do not become so professionally involved. Because they are not so dependent on their occupation or income they do not try to compete for the best jobs, and they often work part-time, or temporarily, to adjust to family demands.

The Two-Career Pattern
The fact is that it is women who move, quit, take part-time work, or fail to compete for promotions in order to lessen conflict with marital and family roles. Even in the case of women who actually are engaged in full-time *careers*, in the usually accepted sense of the term, a certain difficulty in role definition and conflict is the rule. In her study of twenty professional couples sociologist Lynda Lytle Holmstrom found that although compromise was the general rule in deciding on place of residence and occupational mobility, compromises tended to be of the sort where a man took a position while making sure there was a job for his wife. Her career influenced his career decisions, but usually the wife made the career sacrifices when choosing where to live. Most of the husbands *assisted* at least part of the time with housework, and the solution for the problem of child care was for the husband to *help*, for the wife to modify her schedule, or for the couple to hire help. However, despite the attempt of these most enlightened couples to more evenly allocate household responsibilities, it was clear that the husband was *helping out* (never completely sharing) with tasks which still seemed to be defined as those of the wife. This two-career pattern, where both members of the marital pair are characterized by

full-time commitment and dedication, is a far cry from the pattern in which the wife's career is definitely secondary. Rather than working out fairly smoothly, as Paloma's career-secondary pattern was said to operate, the two-career family is considered to be relatively unstable and likely to end in divorce or in the woman giving up (or partially giving up) her career.[51]

The family in which there are two full-time, professional careers of equal importance is uncommon in America and does not appear to be a viable alternative for most families. As described by Helen Papanek, the "two-person career," in which both husband and wife participate in the single career of the husband, is the more typical solution in America. With this pattern, the problem of inequality in occupational opportunities is eliminated, as the aspirations of the highly educated woman are derailed into aspirations for the success of her husband's career. Because of the preference for this pattern, most women either do not prepare themselves at all for a career, or plan on a lesser commitment to an occupation that may necessitate mobility.

Most young women are afraid to commit themselves too deeply to a career or training before they have made their decisions about husband and children so many young women choose careers which will fit in best with family plans—as nurses, teachers, and social workers— or in occupations which can be carried out in the home, such as accounting. Women often do plan their lives around future marriage and family, do drop out of school for marriage, do limit their aspirations, and do abandon careers. Preparing for a career may interfere with a woman's chances for marriage, as success in a career, while a selling point for men, does not enhance a woman's success in the marriage market.

An attitude which holds the family as primary and a career as secondary may be a reasonable, healthy solution, or it may be oppressive and damaging to women. It seems that the "family as primary" approach represents a barrier to true equality as long as only women make the contingency plans. Married women clearly are at a disadvantage in the job or educational area where a role conflict interferes with their success as a worker or as a student. For example, one study shows married women graduate students suffer more than unmarried and divorced students, and achieve the least.[52] Another study demonstrates that unmarried status is related to higher earnings for women, possibly because unmarried women are more likely to have prepared and planned for future occupations.[53] A study of the productivity and success of women faculty members indicated that the married women were taken even less seriously than the single women in terms of belief in their career commitment.[54] The married woman often seems to be in a double-bind in that she is either criticized for not being a good wife and mother, or for not being sufficiently devoted to her career.

The Best of Both Worlds

On the other hand, the woman who successfully combines full-time satisfying work and a successful family life with much role sharing may well have the best of both worlds, and so may her husband. As increasing numbers of commentators are pointing out, perhaps the "rat race" of complete absorption in career is not an appropriate goal for either sex. A less complete commitment to work, allowing for other outlets and pursuits, may be more human, and the demanding, rigorous, dominant nature of a career may be undesirable for anyone. Not all women are willing to invest the time and dedication required for a high-powered career. "Career success demands qualities that are precisely opposite to those demanded for family life,"[55] says Bernard, suggesting the need to de-emphasize or redefine careers. "The career woman is required to order her life in complete conformity to the demands of her profession and to pay whatever price is exacted for deviation from them."[56] Thus the path which may seem best for the individual in terms of psychological and emotional development may be at odds with the most direct path to career success. As long as career success is measured by current standards, and women are expected to adjust their own plans to those of children and husbands, there is little possibility for equal achievement.

ALTERNATIVE FORMS OF MARRIAGE

If the present form of the nuclear family with its division of labor and functions is not ideal for today's needs, some other form or forms must replace or supplement outmoded forms. Although homosexual marriage, celibacy, and non-marriage exist and will continue to do so, at the present time they cannot be said to represent a viable, large-scale substitute for the family.

Other solutions include the idea of day care for the children of working mothers. While day care can be very helpful to a good many women, and will help solve some problems of isolation and economic dependence, day care skirts the issue of sharing of child care or of genuine equality of familial roles.[57] Others have suggested various methods of sharing in child care. Olof Palmé has discussed various government policies in Sweden to lessen sex role stereotypes and increase the father's participation in childrearing.[58] One possibility is "androgynous roles" with women more career-minded and men more family-oriented.[59]

Another suggestion has included the idea of communal living, or living in large extended households, or designing communities where more facilities and functions could be shared. Various forms of communities, communes, and cooperative households already exist or have existed and may relieve participants of some of the stresses of the isolated nuclear family. However, a communal way of living does not necessarily mean equality of sex roles. In Bennett Berger's sample, children were typically almost exclusively in the care of their mothers.[60] Other studies have shown that the Israeli kibbutz came to be divided along sex lines with regard to child care, labor and decision-making.[61] Counterculture marriages, despite overt unconventionality as in the division of functions, often masked an underlying conventionality about status and importance.[62]

The concept of dual-career families has already been discussed in some detail, and is regarded by some as the wave of the future. If both careers are high-powered, however, this has not been found to be a reasonable solution. Another suggestion is that of the shared-role pattern, where each person works half-time and cares for the children and home half-time. The idea of genuinely shared household care and child care is a degree less extreme than the idea of role reversal, where the husband stays at home and the wife becomes bread-winner. No one of these alternatives is suggested as a better form of marriage than the present normative form, but various alternatives might be solutions for different people.

There is, then, nothing in human nature that favors one kind of marriage over any other, none more natural than any other. Whatever we are used to seems natural; anything else, unnatural.[63]

CONCLUSION
Although critics of marriage see it as unworkable, untenable, and stifling to individual development, there is no evidence that other arrangements are better. The conflicts and dissatisfactions within any social structure give rise to change and to new patterns, which in turn generate their own dissatisfactions. Thus, we can expect marriage to continue to evolve and change with changing technological developments and societal requirements and beliefs, but it is unlikely that we will ever develop the perfect and satisfying form. We do, however, wish to know what implications the family form has for equality of roles and development, and we wish to know under what conditions marriages are more (or less) stable. In some ways, we now expect more of marriage than ever before in history, in terms of companionship and psychic support, and yet we become anxious when we see that marriages fail at increasing rates. The rearing of children is too important a task to dismiss the family or the nurturing role as one which is oppressive to women, and there are obviously many rewards involved in parenting.

There is no reason to insist that all marriages *should* be totally equalitarian in that there is complete sharing and even reversal of roles. These marriages, after all, are the most difficult in terms of decision-making about whose career or goals take precedence. However, this form of marriage should be a recognized alternative, and each marriage should be worked out on the basis of the desires and strengths and abilities of both members. Thus in one family the husband will have the career, the wife will act as homemaker and/or have a secondary occupation; in another both will have careers or equally important occupations and both will share in housekeeping and childrearing; and in a third, the wife will act as the major breadwinner with a career commitment, and the husband can assume the homemaker role or have a secondary and subordinate occupation which he can give up easily or move from one place to another as her career plans dictate. These different patterns are not necessarily *equal,* and it would seem from research evidence that the rigid division of labor with one partner as breadwinner-only and the other as homemaker-only may be potentially damaging to both. However, this pattern continues to exist and it may be viable to some.

The essential point is that the failure to provide these alternatives to women (and to men) does limit their capacities. And so we have returned to our initial point, which is that the traditional narrowly defined role of women in marriage and the family is oppressive to women:

> *The diagnosis of the family as the major roadblock to the full emancipation of women is very old. It has been monotonously documented ever since the first industrial revolution. Even before Marx it was recognized as wasteful to the economy as well as limiting to women.* [64]

And thus the family is the target, not for destruction, but for change.

NOTES

1. Shulamith Firestone, *The Dialectic of Sex* (New York: William Morrow, 1970), p. 72.
2. Ibid., p. 205.
3. Juliet Mitchell, *Woman's Estate* (New York: Vintage, 1973), p. 107.
4. Simone de Beauvoir, *The Second Sex,* ed. and trans. H. M. Parshley, (New York: Alfred A. Knopf, Inc., 1970), p. 493.
5. Talcott Parsons and R. F. Bales, *Family, Socialization and Interaction Process* (Glencoe, Ill.: The Free Press, 1955).
6. Daniel R. Miller and Guy E. Swanson, *The Changing American Parent* (New York: John Wiley and Sons, 1958).
7. Jessie Bernard, *The Future of Marriage* (New York: Bantam, 1973), pp. 141–143. Copyright © 1971 by Jessie Bernard from *The Future of Marriage* by Jessie Bernard with permission of World Publishing Company.
8. John Scanzoni, *Sexual Bargaining, Power Politics in the American Marriage* (Englewood Cliffs, N.J.: Prentice-Hall, 1972).
9. John Scanzoni, *Opportunity and the Family* (New York: The Free Press, 1970).
10. Robert O. Blood, Jr., and P. M. Wolfe, *Husbands and Wives* (New York: The Free Press, 1960).
11. Lois Hoffman, "Effects of the Employment of Mothers on Parental Power Relations and the Division of Household Tasks," in *The Employed Women in America,* Ivan Nye and Lois Hoffman (Chicago: Rand-McNally, 1963), pp. 215–230.
12. William H. Chafe, *The American Woman* (London: Oxford University Press, 1972), p. 221.

13. U.S. Bureau of the Census, *Statistical Abstract of the United States, 1975,* 96th ed. (Washington, D.C.: Govt. Printing Office, 1975).

14. Institute of Life Insurance, *Selected Findings from National Survey Research Services,* New York, Spring 1974.

15. Susan Orden and Norman Bradburn, "Working Wives and Marriage Happiness," *American Journal of Sociology* 74 (1969), pp. 392–408.

16. Robert O. Blood, Jr., "The Husband-Wife Relationship," in Nye and Hoffman, 1963, op. cit., pp. 282–305; and "Long-Range Causes and Consequences of Employment of Married Women," *Journal of Marriage and Family* 27 (February 1965), pp. 43–47.

17. Constantina Safilios-Rothschild, *Toward a Sociology of Women* (Lexington, Mass.: Xerox Publishing Company, 1972), p. 69.

18. Eleanor Maccoby, "Effects upon Children of Their Mothers' Outside Employment," in *Work in the Lives of Married Women,* National Manpower Council (New York: Columbia University Press, 1958).

19. Melvin E. Spiro, *Children of the Kibbutz* (Cambridge, Mass.: Harvard University Press, 1958), chapter 16.

20. Lois Hoffman, "Effects on Children: Summary and Discussion," in Nye and Hoffman, 1963, op. cit.

21. Marion R. Yarrow et al., "Childrearing in Families of Working and Non-Working Mothers," *Sociometry* 25 (June 1962), pp. 121–140.

22. Gladys E. Harbeson, *Choice and Challenge for the American Woman,* rev. ed. (Cambridge, Mass.: Schenkman, 1971), reporting on John Bowlby, M.D., *Maternal Care and Mental Health* (Geneva: World Health Org. Monograph No. 2, 1952), pp. 15, 53, 73.

23. Rochelle Wortis, "The Acceptance of the Concept of the Maternal Role by Behavioral Scientists: Its Effect on Women," *American Journal of Orthopsychiatry* 41 (1971), pp. 733–745.

24. Bernard, 1973, op. cit., p. 76.

25. Ibid., p. 170.

26. De Beauvoir, 1970, op. cit., pp. 492, 494.

27. Ibid., p. 463.

28. Elizabeth Janeway, *Man's World, Woman's Place* (New York: Delta, 1971), p. 151.

29. Blood, 1965, op. cit.

30. Ernest W. Burgess, Harvey J. Locke, and Mary Margaret Thomes, *The Family: From Institution to Companionship,* third ed. (New York: American Book Co., 1963).

31. See especially Bernard, 1973, op. cit., pp. 35–57.

32. Jessie Bernard, *Women and the Public Interest* (New York: Aldine Publishing Company, 1971), p. 75.

33. Pat Mainardi, "The Politics of Housework," in *Sisterhood is Powerful,* ed. Robin Morgan (New York: Vintage, 1970), pp. 447–454.

34. Mitchell, 1973, op. cit.

35. Janeway, 1971, op. cit.

36. Sheila Rowbotham, *Woman's Consciousness, Man's World* (New York: Penguin, 1973), pp. 69, 76.

37. De Beauvoir, 1970, op. cit., p. 451.

38. See, for instance: Susan Jacoby, "What Do I Do for the Next 20 Years?" in *Intimacy, Family and Society,* Arlene Skolnick and Jerome Skolnick (Boston: Little, Brown, 1974), pp. 226–236; Mirra Komarovsky, *Blue Collar Marriage* (New York: Vintage, 1967).

39. E. W. Burgess and Paul Wallin, *Engagement and Marriage* (Philadelphia: Lippincott, 1953).

40. Bernard, 1973, op. cit.

41. See Bernard, 1973, op. cit.; Phyllis Chesler, *Women and Madness* (New York: Doubleday, 1972); Walter R. Gove and Jeannette F. Tudor, "Adult Sex Roles and Mental Illness," *American Journal of Sociology* 78 (1973), pp. 50–73.

42. Walter Gove, "The Relationship between Sex Roles, Marital Status, and Marital Illness," *Social Forces* 51 (September 1972), pp. 34–44.

43. Betty Friedan, *The Feminine Mystique* (New York: Dell, 1963).

44. Constantina Safilios-Rothschild and Basil Georgopoulos, "A Comparative Study of Parental and Filial Roles," *Journal of Marriage and Family* (August 1970); also Komarovsky, 1967, op. cit.

45. Komarovsky, 1967, op. cit.; also Lee Rainwater, Richard P. Coleman, and Gerald Handel, *Workingman's Wife* (New York: Oceana, 1959).

46. Jacoby, 1974, op. cit.

47. Janeway, 1971, op. cit., p. 186.

48. Ibid., p. 256.

49. See, for instance: Margaret M. Poloma, "Role Conflict and the Married Professional Woman," in Safilios-Rothschild, 1972, op. cit.

50. Margaret M. Poloma and T. Neal Garland, "The Married Professional Woman: A Study in the Tolerance of Domestication," *Journal of Marriage and Family* 33 (August 1971), pp. 531–540.

51. Lynda Lytle Holmstrom, *The Two Career Family* (Cambridge, Mass.: Schenckman, 1972).

52. Saul D. Feldman, "Impediment or Stimulant? Marital Status and Graduate Education," *American Journal of Sociology* 78 (1973), pp. 220–232.

53. Elizabeth M. Havens, "Women, Work and Wedlock: A Note on Female Marital Patterns in the United States," *American Journal of Sociology* 78 (1973), pp. 213–219.

54. Marianne A. Ferber and Jane W. Loeb, "Performance, Rewards, and Perceptions of Sex Discrimination among Male and Female Faculty," *American Journal of Sociology* 78 (1973), pp. 233–240.

55. Bernard, 1971, op. cit.

56. Ibid., p. 180.

57. Rosalyn Baxandall, "Who Shall Care for Our Children? The History and Development of Day Care in the United States," in *Women: A Feminist Perspective*, ed. Jo Freeman (Palo Alto, Calif.: Mayfield, 1975), pp. 88–101; Louise Gross and Phyllis MacEwan, "On Day Care," in *Liberation Now!*, ed. Deborah Babcox and Madeline Belkin (New York: Dell, 1971), pp. 123–131; Peggy and Peter Steinfels, "Day Care: Patchwork, Realization, or Utopia?" in Skolnick and Skolnick, 1974, op. cit.

58. Olof Palme, "The Emancipation of Man," in Skolnick and Skolnick, 1974, op. cit.

59. Alice Rossi, "Equality Between the Sexes: An Immodest Proposal," in *The Woman in America*, ed. R. J. Lifton (Boston: Beacon Press, 1964), pp. 98–143.

60. Bennett M. Berger, Bruce M. Hackett, and R. Mervyn Millar, "Child-Rearing Practices in the Communal Family," in Skolnick and Skolnick, 1974, op. cit., pp. 441–463.

61. Spiro, 1958, op. cit.

62. John S. Kafka and Robert C. Ryder, "Notes on Marriages in the Counter Culture," in Skolnick and Skolnick, 1974, op. cit., pp. 304–312.

63. Bernard, 1973, op. cit., p. 307.

64. Bernard, 1971, op. cit., p. 258.

ADDITIONAL REFERENCES

1. Andreas, Carol. *Sex and Caste in America*. Englewood Cliffs, N.J.: Prentice-Hall, 1971, p. 63.

2. Angrist, Shirley. "The Study of Sex Roles." *Journal of Social Issues* 25, 1969.

3. Bart, Pauline. "Depression in Middle-Aged Women." *Woman in Sexist Society*. ed. Vivian Gornick and Barbara K. Moran. New York: Basic Books, 1971, pp. 163–186.

4. Bernard, Jessie. *Academic Women*. University Park: Pennsylvania State University, 1964.

5. Bibbington, A. C. "The Function of Stress in the Establishment of the Dual-Career Family." *Journal of Marriage and Family* 35, 1973, pp. 530–538.

6. Bird, Carolyn. *Born Female*. rev. ed. New York: Pocket Books, 1971.

7. Blau, Peter. *Exchange and Power in Social Life*. New York: John Wiley and Sons, 1964, p. 301.

8. Brown, Judith. "A Note on the Division of Labor by Sex." *Intimacy, Family and Society*. ed. Arlene Skolnick and Jerome Skolnick. Boston: Little, Brown, 1974.

9. Brownmiller, Susan. "Sisterhood Is Powerful." *New York Times Magazine* 15, March 1970, p. 140.

10. Duberman, Lucile. *Marriage and its Alternatives*. New York: Praeger, 1974, p. 199.

11. Epstein, Cynthia Fuchs. *Woman's Place*. Berkeley: University of California Press, 1971, p. 112.

12. Gough, Kathleen. "The Origin of the Family." *Journal of Marriage and Family*, November 1971, pp. 760–771.

13. Janeway, Elizabeth. *Man's World, Woman's Place*. New York: Delta, 1971.

14. Levinger, George. "Task and Social Behavior in Marriage." *Sociometry* 27, December 1964, pp. 433–448.

15. Litwak, Eugene. "Technological Innovation and Ideal Form of Family Structure in an Industrial Democratic Society." *Families in East and West*. ed. Reuben Hill and Rene Koenig, Socialization Process and Kinship Ties, The Hague: Mouton and Co., 1970.

16. Nye, F. I. "Emerging and Declining Family Roles." *Journal of Marriage and Family* 36, 1974, pp. 238–246, for a discussion of the new responsibilities and functions of today's family.

17. Papanek, Helen. "Men, Women and Work: Reflections on the Two-Person Career." *American Journal of Sociology* 78, 1973, pp. 852–873.

18. Rapoport, Rhona and Robert. *Dual Career Families*. Baltimore: Penguin Books, 1971.

19. Reiss, Ira L. *The Family System in America*. New York: Holt, Rinehart and Winston, 1971.

20. Slater, Philip. *The Pursuit of Loneliness*. Boston: Beacon Press, 1970.

21. Slater, Philip. "Parental Role Differentiation." *American Journal of Sociology* 67, 1961, pp. 296–312.

22. Syfers, Judy. "I Want a Wife." *The First Ms. Reader*. New York: Warner Paperbacks, 1973.

23. U.S. Dept. of Health, Education and Welfare, National Center for Health Statistics. *Vital Statistics of the United States, 1970*. Vol. II, section 5, Life Tables, Rockville, Md.: Public Health Service, Health Resources Administration, 1970.

3
OUR EDUCATIONAL INSTITUTIONS

Girls are trained to be responders, boys to be initiators.

—*Carl Couch*

Over half a century ago, Charlotte Perkins Gilman wrote that there was an androcentric bias in education, based on the assumption that only men were fully human and only they needed to know of the world and how to run it.[1] However, even though it is no longer fashionable to speak of only men as worthy of being educated, a number of ideas about why women should not be educated still survive. From Aristotle, who felt women should not be educated at all because they lack deliberation, temperance, fortitude and justice, we "progressed" to the stage where it was considered acceptable to educate women. However, it was acceptable only if such education suited their role definition and usefulness to men, as too much education for women would only lead to trouble. To those who believe in this limited concept, women are considered teachable, but only just; basically they are inferior in intellect to men and unreliable emotionally. A slightly more "advanced" view is that education is acceptable for women because it makes a woman more pleasing to a husband, as she is more cultivated and able to carry on an interesting conversation.

From a personal communication to the author from Carl Couch, in 1974.

The truly enlightened view—hardly modern in that it was stated by Plato and elaborated by John Stuart Mill—is that both sexes should be educated equally and according to their individual preferences and proclivities. Mill, while not believing women to be inferior, stated the currently popular opinion that we cannot know the nature of the two sexes as long as artificial patterns and expectations mold them. The "natures" which appeared to be natural in Mills' time were, he stated, a result of forced repression and unnatural stimulation.[2] While not ignoring the possibility that there are innate biological differences between the sexes on such characteristics as level of aggression, the enlightened view is simply based on the reality that we *do not know,* because there is presently no way to separate the effects of the inherent characteristics from those which are learned and culturally molded.

INTELLIGENCE AND SEX

A number of researchers have dealt with the issue of female intelligence and have concluded that (1) the sex differences which appear to be found in such areas as verbal and mathematical ability are small and (2) there is far more difference between people of the same sex than between the two sexes.[3] If there *are* inborn differences in intelligence—and this has never been clearly demonstrated—they are very small and by no means dichotomize the sexes into "intelligent" and "nonintelligent." All *apparent sex differences* in intelligence *may* be explained by early learning and continual cumulative reinforcement. There is a possibility that there are certain innate differences between the sexes which contribute to different patterns of learning and performance. The most commonly studied and carefully documented of these possible differences is aggression.

Males do appear to be the more aggressive sex, in a wide variety of settings and using many different ways of measuring aggression. This conclusion is based on observations of children in natural settings, behavior following exposure to models in experimental settings, parents' descriptions of their children's behavior, peer ratings on aggressive behavior items, greater aggressive content in responses to projective tests and scales or questionnaires, and activity level during play. It is not clear whether differences in level of aggression are learned and encouraged or whether they have a biological base, but the fact that females are not more aggressive than males in any known society for which reliable evidence is available, and the fact that increasing the level of male hormones increases aggressive behavior, does give some weight to the argument for a biological difference.[4] Restraints on the intellectuality of girls begin early and have the effect of depressing their initially higher verbal and language skills. This may be at least partly accomplished by differences in independence training. Boys are encouraged to develop problem-solving orientations earlier than girls and are encouraged to become independent and to meet challenges. Boys develop a problem-solving, decision-making, active approach to everyday life, whereas girls tend not to act on the environment until it has acted upon them. Therefore, intellectual differences may be a combination of differences in physical factors present at birth, the way children are dealt with by the adults responsible for their care, and the social roles children know they are preparing for. Later conflicting interests and responsibilities may simply add to the effects of these early patterns.

Educational institutions, along with other major institutions such as the family, help to create and define reality for their charges, to perpetuate the definition of reality which exists, and to reinforce the stereotypes and myths which characterize our culture.

At school, young male and female students are expected to be two very different sorts of beings. The school nurtures and reinforces the "natural" proclivities of females and males, thereby perpetuating the norms and expectations of the existing social order. The perceived differences, based on traditional views of female and male roles, maintain the status quo and channel persons into the different roles and tasks which must be performed for the maintenance of society. Just as it has been argued that social stratification is "functional" for maintaining the social system, so it is "functional" to train approximately half the human race for breadwinning and the other half for emotional support functions and for performing the daily chores of family life. This system works fairly well as long as people can be convinced of the rightness and "naturalness" of their assigned spheres and as long as they are so thoroughly channeled by the institutions of society that they are unable to question it. Although there obviously have been failures of and exceptions to this channeling, the schools have helped to maintain sexism in American society. Far from acting as agents of social change, educational institutions act as agents of social control, perpetuating myths and stereotypes and maintaining the status quo.

Textbooks, curriculum, and classroom practices also tend to reinforce existing sex stereotypes and indeed almost to omit women altogether. The best studies of children's textbooks and readers all show that women and girls, until very recently, have been depicted far less often than men and boys, and rarely in major roles; that professional or "successful" female role models are all but nonexistent; and that women and girls are presented as passive, dependent, nonachieving, and limited in possible roles. Researchers have found that women constitute 20–30 percent of human and animal representations in children's books.[5] The American Library Association list of Notable Books for Children for 1969 lists two books about boys to every one about girls. Boys were portrayed as independent, competent human beings who do many exciting things, while girls were pictured as helping with domestic chores or passively watching the boys.[6] By 1975, the Notable Books for Children seems to have changed considerably, so that there were almost equal numbers of books which had male main characters (15) and female main characters (14). Without reading each of the books no further comparisons are possible, but the descriptions of the books indicate that they seem to avoid sex stereotyping.[7]

Even animal stories depict male and female animals in traditionally stereotyped ways, and fairy tales depict women as either the beautiful and helpless princess, or the ugly and usually evil witch. Others have found that math books also stereotype masculine and feminine roles and discriminate against females. In addition to the differential activities of boys and girls in arithmetic books, Florence Howe found other textbooks also at fault: six picture-rich science textbooks showed only three pictures of women, and social studies textbooks were not only negligent about portraying important women in the history of the country, but failed to reflect the reality of women as they participate in the labor force and other aspects of society.

Although sex stereotyping in curriculum and textbooks is undergoing tremendous change, the fact is that all of the legislation, court challenges, and publishers' guidelines have arisen in the past few years. In 1976, books that depict women or girls only in subordinate roles can be and are being removed from the shelves. New books are being written in which roles are being expanded and language is being changed. McGraw-Hill Publishing Company, for instance, has developed a project called "Guidelines for Equal Treatment of the Sexes." It is available to all publishers and suggests ways in which they can eliminate sex stereotyping, for instance by showing married women working outside the home and treating this favorably. Other suggestions are to emphasize that women have choices about marital status, just as men do; to not imply that the emotional life of a family suffers when women work outside the home; and to show both men and women in various household tasks. However, despite the fact that Title IX of the Civil Rights Act outlaws blatant sexism in textbooks, and despite the fact that task forces in most states are working on implementing the necessary changes, sexism does remain. The examination of the Iowa Special Committee on Sex Stereotyping in Education in 1975 of junior high textbooks still found males vastly outnumbering females, and girls were still often depicted as passive and scared.[8]

Curriculum

Research into the area of curriculum has shown that, from the beginning, boys and girls have not been treated alike with regard to subject matter and areas of interest. Girls have been supposed to like reading and hate math and science, and were encouraged in those directions. Different fields have been emphasized so early in the educational process that children may not have considered the possibility of becoming interested in a de-emphasized subject. Some curriculum and classroom segregations have been quite explicit, for instance, when enrollment in home economics is restricted to girls and shop or industrial arts to boys. Although these restrictions are no longer legal, the sex-typing of classes remains, especially in such areas as vocational agriculture courses, and consumer and homemaking courses, according to the National Education Association's own Educational Research Survey. Even more important to many is discrimination in physical education and sports, where activities and facilities are often segregated by sex, and allocations to boys' programs are much greater than those for girls. While sex segregation itself may be bad enough because it encourages an attitude of non-cooperation and belief that the sexes *cannot* participate together in sports, it also usually means that girls' physical education is of a very different order from that of boys'. Where boys' physical education emphasizes team games, large muscle activity, and development of both cooperation and competition, girls' physical education is often less active, more "graceful," oriented to figure exercises and easy sports, with less emphasis on team effort and competition.

Classroom Practices
Even class chores or assignments are usually sex-typed. Boys do the carrying or moving of furniture and desks, while girls set the tables and put out refreshments. There is often explicit sex segregation in lines, seating arrangements, in teams for spelling bees, and for almost every other activity, regardless of the necessity for such practices.[9] Differences are also allowed on the basis of sex for noise, aggression, and physical activity, with boys being allowed greater leeway, since it is their "nature" to be loud and boisterous. Not the least important, offices of clubs and classes often are sex-linked, with fewer girls being elected to offices, or when they are elected, commonly holding secondary or secretarial positions, rather than the leading positions.

Although it is obvious that many of the practices described above are undergoing change, that many educators are advocating "open education" (which propounds nonsexism to students and student teachers),[10] the important point is not what is now changing, but what forces have shaped those of us who are now adults. The schools have, in the past, been one of the important agents in socializing children into "appropriate" roles, thus, the schools are now an appropriate target for change.

Attitudes of Teachers
It is now widely accepted that teachers' expectations of children influence their performances. The effects of teacher expectations are not entirely clear, as different studies have shown that manipulating expectancies sometimes produces the expected outcome, sometimes

does not, and sometimes backfires.[11] Some studies indicate that teachers do have preconceptions of children based on characteristics such as social class, neatness, attractiveness, and sex. With the recent interest in reducing sexism in the schools, teachers have been made more aware of their own attitudes and behavior and how they can work to eliminate sexism. This is especially important, as teachers tend to communicate their expectancies and preconceptions to children in subtle ways. Research on the "interaction quality hypothesis" suggests that teachers vary the quality of their relationships with students depending on their expectations of them.[12] However, apparently not all children are equally sensitive to the teachers' expectations, so expectations do not always lead to different behavior.

A study of pre-kindergarten teachers showed that many believe boys and girls are naturally different in aggression and passivity. Because of their beliefs, these teachers tend to reinforce these different behaviors in children. Schools may actually have to do *more* than treat children equally—they may have to compensate for already existing limitations by encouraging children in areas in which they might not ordinarily be encouraged.[13]

Research has indicated that there are differences in interpersonal interaction between teachers and boys and teachers and girls. Whether or not the influence of the teacher is "feminizing," apparently the teacher is directing more of her or his attention to boys, in terms of praise, encouragement, and instruction, as well as of criticism and reprimands.[14]

Patricia Sexton argues that boys are the more damaged by the schools' "feminizing tendencies" which suppress and distort "normal male impulses." However, the qualities she refers to as "masculine" are those which are desirable in both sexes (such as autonomy and independence). Sexton states that the *male* temperament is nourished by the freedom to dissent, to state one's own opinion, to make decisions for oneself. Don't these freedoms nourish the *human* temperament? Sexton seems to imply that it is acceptable to repress girls, but tragic to repress boys.[15]

The "feminizing" aspects of the schools are often overemphasized, ignoring the fact that curriculum materials emphasize males and male activities, and that far from being inhibited in aggression, boys are often forced to *prove* themselves in sports, to prove themselves *not* "sissies." As Clarice Stasz Stoll has put it, "If schools are hard on boys, it is in insisting upon their performing according to rigid middle-class views of masculinity, not in feminizing them."[16] The present interest is not in analyzing the effect of the educational institutions on males, or even on all children, but specifically on girls. The cumulative effects of some relatively minor and some major types of sex stereotyping are potentially great, particularly when they reinforce messages being received from various other sources. Consider these differences at three levels of education: early schooling; high school; and higher education.

EARLY SCHOOLING

The staff of elementary schools, in terms of sex composition, attitudes, and actions about boys and girls, show patterns of sex differentiation. About 88 percent of elementary school teachers are women, but only 22 percent of the elementary principals and administrators.[17] Even so, it is not unknown that women teachers in the early grades perpetuate the idea that men are better than women at everything and that women really ought to be in the home. However, it is not even necessary that women teachers hold any anti-feminine bias, because despite the fact that teachers *feel* they treat all students fairly and equally, researchers have found evidence of differential evaluations of students according to different expectations which could be based on sex-role stereotypes.[18] A study done in New York City showed that teachers wanted males to be dominant, independent, and assertive, while they preferred that females be submissive, unassertive, and concerned about their appearance.[19] Another study found that two-thirds of teachers agreed to at least some extent that "most women have only themselves to blame for not doing better in life," which could be indicative of an overall anti-feminine bias.[20]

In particular, early schooling controls and inhibits behavior by demanding and reinforcing qualities of conformity, docility, and dependence, while at the same time expecting achievement and a certain amount of competition, especially for boys. Although this may create a bewildering situation of conflict for the boy, it is no better for the girl, as the messages to conform and be obedient simply reinforce the image of girls that is presented elsewhere in the culture. Although the schools don't create the roles, they exert a powerful and limiting influence by defining specific attitudes, actions, and opportunities appropriate for girls and boys.

In a general way, schools stunt the ability of the child to choose how to behave and think in accordance with her or his own needs and wishes, by assigning children to roles based on their gender. Different expectations regarding their sex-differentiated skills, natures, and interests lead girls to be channeled toward reading and sedentary activities, to music and art, while boys are channeled toward mechanical and physical activities, to math and science. Even in schools designed to be progressive, open, and enlightened, a considerable amount of sex-stereotyped socialization occurs.

"As feminists see it, schools—institutions for socialization within a sexist society—in spite of good intentions, mold children willy-nilly according to societal notions of acceptable behavior."[21]

One School's Attempt to Eradicate Sexism
In an excellent analysis by Barbara Grizzuti Harrison of the attempt of one school to "unlearn the lie" that girls are innately passive, unaggressive, supportive and domestic, their nature being to need, to want, and to wait, the conclusion was that messages about sex expectations are daily and unremitting, and although in themselves relatively trivial, when taken cumulatively articulate a world-view. A Sex-roles Committee was formed in this school to eradicate sexism so as to make both sexes more fully human, more fully aware of the options available to them. The committee felt that the important thing was to put back the options that had already been squeezed out by the time children were eight or nine. What these concerned parents wanted was not an emphasis on discrimination and prejudice against girls, but a new awareness of some of the ways in which women are oppressed. What the parents wanted for their female children was exactly what parents tend to want for their male children—independence, resourcefulness, assertiveness, and recognition of options available to them. Differential treatment, expectations, and goals for boys and girls therefore had to be eliminated before anything approaching equality of education could be hoped for.

Curriculum materials and library resources were to be revamped so as to reflect the experiences of women, teach the history of women, and develop a skills-resource bank which could call on women for contributions as speakers and as role models for children in the school.

The goal of this group was not limited and its scope not narrow. The approach required a great deal of effort and agonizing, and underwent various setbacks. However, despite the difficulties of such a major overhaul of the early educational institutions, this is exactly what is required before meaningful changes can be expected to take place at any later point in the educational process.

LATER SCHOOLING: HIGH SCHOOL
Many of the processes occurring in early schooling can also prevail in the high school. In high school, many sorts of sex-segregated activities become even more pronounced in their segregation patterns; for instance, in channeling coursework and planning for future occupations.

High school girls often join "future homemaker" clubs and pep clubs, while boys join math and science clubs. Boys are expected to be athletes or to help manage the athletic teams, while girls tend to join the pep squad, drill team, and drum majorettes. The boys perform, the girls cheer. The boys' athletic programs are given ample funding and much publicity, while the girls' sports activities are, by and large, ignored. The stereotype of the muscular and virile male athlete emerges, opposed to that of the cute and exuberantly feminine cheerleader. The gap widens.

All school activities seem to solidify the sexes into their pre-ordained roles, and curriculum materials and coursework are certainly no less sexist, no more reflective of the contributions of women to society than were the materials in elementary school. Classes such as those in math and science become even more solidly sex-segregated as girls move away from these fields. Most high school history texts omit many women of importance. When women are included, it is often in a separate section, and the barriers these women faced are minimized. This reinforces the idea that women of note are optional and supplementary. This is probably not an intentional bias, but simply reflects the attitude that male activities are more important.[22]

Counselors are criticized by feminists for their tendency to guide female students into "feminine" occupations and channel them into "feminine" courses. They also often assume that all girls desire marriage and family above all and will plan their educations and occupations around their future husbands and children. Counselors will defend these practices on the basis of what girls "realistically" have to face, which becomes the excuse for maintaining the status quo. This approach will assure another generation of people unprepared for anything other than sex-stereotyped occupations.[23] High school girls who had job counseling were more likely to select office work and the role of housewife than were those with no counseling.[24] Counseling becomes merely "an institutionalized means of defending the existing social order," by steering girls into safe, especially clerical, jobs.[25]

In "On De-segregating Stuyvesant High," Alice de Rivera described her high school experience. She explained that she first realized her own oppression when she became aware that she had no plans for the future. When she tried to correct this by preparing to enter a scientific field, she found that the specialized science and math high schools were for males only. Most of the vocational high schools were overwhelmingly male also, and taught trades in electronics, carpentry, plumbing, foods, and printing. When they entered special vocational schools, girls were trained as health aides, in cosmetology, secretarial skills, nursing, cooking and fashion design. High school girls were not encouraged to take the "masculine" vocational courses even when vocational high schools were coeducational. On the effects of sex-segregation on the relationship between the sexes, de Rivera concluded:

> The psychological result of the school which is segregated by sex —only because of tradition —is to impress upon girls that they are only "flighty females" who would bother the boys' study habits (as a consequence of girls not being interested in anything but the male sex). This insinuates immaturity on the part of girls —and certainly produces it in both sexes. A boy who has never worked with a girl in the classroom is bound to think of her as his intellectual inferior. . . . Both sexes learn to deal with each other as non-people.[26]

Yet, the development of interests is served no better by coeducational high schools, where girls find themselves spending a good bit of their time worrying about their hair, their clothes, and how they appear to boys, and fighting for the attention of boys while trying to compete in the popularity arena. The high school seems to be designed to continue those traditions begun in grade school and to strongly reinforce the image of the young woman as attractive and appealing, non-serious, and oriented solely to males. Girls are more constrained by the status system not to hold scholastic achievement as a high value because of the lack of social rewards for having an intellectual orientation.[27]

COLLEGE

Screening for higher education begins as young people enter college, with women students generally entering with lower vocational aspirations. In 1972, although slightly over half (50.6 percent) of all high school diplomas were granted to women, only 40.4 percent of bachelor's or first professional degrees went to women. Even fewer women attained master's degrees (33.8 percent of degrees awarded), and only 11.6 percent obtained doctoral degrees.[28] Pamela Roby has discussed many of the structural barriers, or the organizational patterns and practices which hinder women in obtaining higher education. Among these are admission policies, which often favor male over female applicants on the grounds that females are a poorer risk and investment as they may not graduate. Also, policies which discriminate against older and returning students usually discriminate against women, who are found to be more likely to delay or interrupt their education and return later. The granting of financial aid also may discriminate against women both because female students are regarded as less serious and because they are more often expected to have someone to support them.

Other structural barriers include certain rules, such as those requiring residency in the state for regular tuition, full-time status expectations, and the difficulty of transferring credits from one college to another. These policies discriminate against women in that women are more likely to have had to change campuses, and even states, as they have followed their husbands.

No less important, however, is the subject matter of the courses themselves, and the way in which this material is presented. As women are presented with a male-dominated curriculum, a "masculine" view of the world, and an overwhelmingly male faculty, women may come to believe in the male dominance of all important activities. Evidence from various sources indicates that when women and minorities are presented with a white, middle-class, male view of the world, they begin to limit their own aspirations.

Literature courses require that students read male authors, history courses teach about famous men in history, and even the social sciences curriculum, supposedly the vanguard of social change, presents a view of the world which either does not include women at all or includes them only in their traditionally defined places. Several studies have pointed to the limitations of textbooks available in college courses. One is B. F. Kirschner's study of introductory sociology texts, in which it is concluded that these texts seldom expose students to a systematic analysis of women in society.[29] Still more critical is Carole Ehrlich's survey of marriage and family texts, which she found to be full of myths and folklore about women, presented as facts, and used to justify woman's subordinate status.[30] Child development books have been surveyed and have been found to show a lack of responsiveness to issues widely discussed in the women's movement.[31] Women are not only neglected in textbooks and curriculum, but are not considered as persons in the stratification system, tending to be assigned the status of their husbands or fathers.[32] Sociology has not been a science of society, but of male society, and many of the popular sociological theories (such as functionalism) have served to justify the status quo.[33]

Education for those who are never expected to assume positions of responsibility becomes "ornamental rather than useful."[34] Women in college are caught in a conflict-ridden situation, or a cultural contradiction—do they want to be professionals, or the wives of professionals? Can they resolve the contradiction between traditional and modern roles?[35] Will education be wasted on them if they don't have a career? In addition to the Komarovsky study, which has demonstrated the conflicts in college women over the conflicting messages they receive about achieving in school while being appealing to men, a series of studies by Matina Horner has shown that this conflict situation may be a stressful one which helps to create a "motivation to avoid sucess."[36] Horner's work was based on the observation that many bright college women seemed to be confused and actually fearful about situations of achievement. These college women seemed to be caught in a double bind where "success" in the achievement sphere might mean failure in the feminine sphere. Her studies demonstrated that women showed anxiety over achieving success because they expected negative consequences in terms of social rejection and feelings of being unfeminine. Horner points out that women fear success in a *man's* world, or by a masculine definition of success, rather than displaying a generalized fear of success in *any* sphere. However, since "success" in general ordinarily is equated with success in the (male) occupational world, this definition represents another brake on a woman's ability to attain equality with men in any arena. More recently, some research has shown that the majority of subjects of both sexes showed "fear of success" imagery.[37] It may be that the self-attitudes of both sexes are changing with young women becoming less anxious, young men more anxious over competitive, achievement-oriented situations.

Eleanor Maccoby also has discussed the problem of the effects of "defying convention" on women's personalities:

Suppose a girl does succeed in maintaining, throughout her childhood years, the qualities of dominance, independence, and active striving that appear to be requisites for good analytic thinking. In so doing she is defying the conventions concerning what is appropriate behavior for her sex. She may do this successfully, in many ways, but I suggest that it is a rare intellectual woman who will not have paid a price for it: a price in anxiety. And I hazard the guess that it is this anxiety which helps to account for the lack of productivity among those women who do make intellectual careers.[38]

Social rejection alone, or the fear of it, is enough to discourage competition with men. However, this represents a situation for women not of conflict, but of ambivalence, where women enjoy their feminine identity and qualities and simultaneously perceive them as less important than those of men.[39]

The failure of women to equal men in educational attainment could be blamed on a system which makes it impossible for women to conceive of themselves as achieving. On the other hand, it could be blamed on women themselves who, given all the chances in the world, fail to take full advantage of them. College women's educational ambition in part is to secure husbands through whom they can realize their own ambitions.[40] Thus, college may be only a "hunting ground" for some women, and the cultural enrichment approach to education may seem to be sufficient for those students. This may be a legitimate approach, and perhaps education should not necessarily be limited only to those who are going to "pay society back" for their education by entering the occupational world, whether male or female. However, if some women approach education in a non-serious way, it is no reason to judge all women students as non-serious.

What Should Women Do?

Going to college with the idea of finding a husband and then quitting (a stereotype with some basis in fact) cannot be seen as a very realistic or reasonable thing to do. Women would benefit from staying in school and preparing themselves for some kind of work. Chances are very good that they will have to support themselves at some time in the future—because they remain single, because they are deserted or divorced, because they are widowed, because of insufficient family incomes, or because they need a job to avoid going crazy or losing their sense of identity. There are, of course, still a large number of women (married and well provided for by their husbands) who never will be required to work. However, examination of recent trends in the stability of marriages suggests that it is now less likely that any woman should count on never having to support herself.

Should a woman relegate herself to the least remunerative, least skilled jobs? The choice is not necessarily between a thrilling and glamorous career and a less satisfying occupation, but between employment and unemployment. Women no longer are assured of families who will support them for life nor are they assured of support from former husbands or from grown children. Since many must make their own way, should they not be provided with the tools to do so? These tools include, not necessarily college training, but any skill or vocational training, particularly at the post-high school level, for those women who will probably work at some point in their lives.

For many of the reasons discussed above, the "cultural enrichment" approach to education for women is probably unrealistic and does not meet real needs. It is no longer legitimate to send women to college to be nothing more than more interesting companions for their future husbands. However, our major problem is in getting women and men, faculty and students, to accept women as being completely serious about their career preparation.[41] Almost no one any longer seriously suggests that women not be educated at all, but many continue to suggest that women be educated in culture and the arts, so as to be fine and gracious hostesses, or (on a different socioeconomic level) to prepare themselves with secretarial skills to "fall back on." While both approaches may seem reasonable as long as women are always viewed as adjuncts to men, neither produces women who can be expected to be "successful" in the generally accepted masculine sense.

GRADUATE AND PROFESSIONAL SCHOOLS
Women who have survived the educational system to the point of graduate or professional school obviously represent a selected sample in contemporary society. However, despite the fact that they have already overcome a number of barriers, have escaped some of the oppressive aspects of their early socialization experiences, and have developed aspirations unusual in young women in our society, they have not yet achieved a state in which it is no longer necessary to prove themselves. On the contrary, women in graduate and professional schools continue to be viewed and treated as non-serious, and possibly worse yet, they may be subjected to bad images of female graduate students based on the notion that they are in graduate school as a compensation for having failed to find a husband. However, the woman graduate student who is not single, and therefore cannot be considered a frustrated female searching for a male,[42] may escape that stereotype while still not being taken seriously. For example, it

may be assumed by faculty that her marital and family responsibilities will outweigh academic ones. Many male faculty members seem to assume that women graduate students are poor risks, especially for financial aid, because they are "more likely to drop out."[43] While it may be true that women tend to drop out at somewhat higher rates than men, it has been my observation that male faculty tend to attribute this failure to emotional or personal problems in women, while for men they are more likely to feel there was a "good" reason, such as the need to earn a living. Male faculty members seem to overlook the fact that women have many excellent reasons for dropping out of school, including especially lack of encouragement and being treated as not committed to the profession. In addition to problems mentioned earlier with regard to actual discrimination in the rewarding of financial aid, or the masculine style and approach of the curriculum, more subtle problems occur on the level of exclusion from some informal social networks. It is much more difficult for a woman graduate student to have informal friendship ties with male faculty members, and harder for her to become part of an informal group from her department who play basketball together, or go drinking together on a regular basis. Although it is possible for a woman to become "one of the boys," she must be very aggressive to do so, and she still risks rejection.

Another tendency of some women in graduate school, impossible for achievement-oriented people to understand, is that they will not compete on the same basis as many men, refusing to accept the "masculine" values of the students and faculty. Thus, when a woman graduate student drops out on ideological or intellectual grounds, the dropout is taken to be a sign of failure on her part—a sign of weakness rather than of strength. While her decision *may* reflect independence and a dedication to principles, it is interpreted more often as a sign of instability, and is often attributed to problems in personal relationships or emotional/psychological problems. It is also still true that women are freer to make the decision to leave school, if only because it is somewhat less likely for women than for men that others are dependent on them for present and future support. More importantly, it is also less a sign of failure for a woman to leave graduate school than it is for a man. While much of a man's identity and ego are bound to his success in school and occupation, a woman is not expected to achieve highly, so she is less stigmatized when she fails to do so.

The woman who does remain in graduate or professional school usually is not only quite serious about a career, but feels she can combine this successfully with marriage. If all else were equal, there would be no reason to assume that this should be any more difficult for the educated woman than for the educated man. Of course, all other things are not equal, and Feldman has shown that the married woman is caught between the conflicts of the two major roles of student and spouse, and suffers most, in terms of success as a graduate student, from this role conflict. The woman in this position is more likely to drop out of graduate school, less likely to engage in anticipatory socialization necessary for preparing for a future academic role, and more likely to have limited opportunities if she *is* able to complete her studies than are other categories of graduate students. Married men studied were not found to have this conflict: they were productive and the best adjusted of all graduate students. The most committed and active graduate students were the divorced women; divorce seemed to be a force for liberation for women as they lost a source of severe role conflict. Divorce was found to be a source of strain for men as they lost a supportive relationship.[44]

The woman graduate student has been pictured as being rather grim, finding herself further and further removed from ordinary roles and pursuits, and less and less involved in pursuing "normal" fulfillment for a woman.[45] She therefore may suffer feelings of rejection from those who disapprove of this course of action. Even without this consideration, women seem to suffer more than men from the "is-it-all worth-it?" syndrome; from always having to prove themselves and their ability; and from always having to convince everyone they are in earnest. These pressures, combined with minimal encouragement and faint praise tinged with condescension (that they are hardworking, neat, systematic, patient), contribute to the likelihood that one day they will decide it is *not* worth it.

Graduate education normally comes at the period of greatest external and internal pressures to assume the traditional roles of wife and mother. Thus, there may be strong conflicts between family and academic obligations, problems with children at home or a husband not supportive of his wife's higher education, and conflicts within the woman herself about the appropriate role for a woman. Is there a conflict between femininity and intellectual achievement? Does she really have sufficient aggression and stamina to succeed? Partly because of the cultural belief in the mutual exclusiveness of femininity and competitive achievement, women have greater self-doubts than do men about their academic ability, despite higher grades. And it is not only self-doubts that are created by this image of women as inferior graduate students, as another consequence is a sort of "identification with the oppressor"—a rejection of women and particularly of women's issues, as a result of the wish to disassociate oneself as much as possible from the negative image. Only in very recent years has this pattern begun to change, and women to have become not only willing but sometimes eager, to identify with other women colleagues, to engage in feminist studies, and to become involved in women's issues.

The picture with regard to graduate and professional education for women has begun to improve, and in fact between 1969–72 and

1972–75, a study of 46 universities in the American Association of Universities showed the small increases in the awarding of doctorates were increases for women and minority students. However, this increase was only from about 15 percent to 21 percent of all Ph.D.s awarded to women, and less than 10 percent of these were in traditionally male fields.[46] Another very complex analysis of admissions data from the University of California at Berkeley demonstrated no bias in the admission system, but concluded that the bias had come from earlier screening which had channeled women into fields that were "generally more crowded, less productive of completed degrees, and less well-funded, and that frequently offer poorer professional employment prospects."[47] Schools of law and medicine also have seen great increases in enrollment of women.[47] Since there are changes in the admission of women to graduate and professional schools, and an increased number of advanced degrees going to women, it is very possible that we will see a change in the labor force in five to ten years as these women move into their professions. However, it is still true that women receive proportionately fewer of the advanced degrees the higher they go.

Table 3-1 Number of doctorates conferred on majority men, majority women, minority men, and minority women, 1969–72 and 1972–75

	1969–72	(% of total)	1972–75	(% of total)	Percent change
Majority men	43,768	(82.1)	39,773	(74.6)	−9
Majority women	7,781	(14.6)	10,451	(19.6)	+34
Minority men	1,332	(2.5)	2,139	(4.0)	+61
Minority women	414	(0.7)	964	(1.8)	+133

Source: Table 2, p. 858, in J. L. McCarthy and D. Wolfe, "Doctorates Granted to Women and Minority Group Members," *Science* 189, No. 4206, 12 September 1975, pp. 856–859. Copyright 1975 by The American Association for the Advancement of Science.

CONCLUSION

Discrimination begins in early grades, continues and is reinforced throughout the educational experience, and eventually is taken, not as oppression of women, but as the social reality of their inabilities in intellectual skills. College and graduate schools could change to reflect greater female input, through courses in women's studies, greater numbers of women as faculty members, and general raising of consciousness about women's issues, as well as making education generally more accessible to persons not easily able to adapt to the structure and rules of the university.

Early education could be changed to improve the societal image of all women, regardless of their eventual educational attainment, and to break down some of the early stereotypes about the possibilities all children—girls and boys alike—have for the future. All young girls should be encouraged to develop a view of themselves as capable of a variety of things, and to be able to think of themselves in a variety of possible future roles. This should be no less true for boys, but it is especially important for girls to learn that there is no need to be in a situation of "cultural contradiction" or conflict, and that they need not think there is incompatibility between learning or intelligence and being feminine. Girls and women should not be encouraged to think of school as a holding pattern, or something to do until they find the right husbands, thus engaging in an activity with no real meaning or purpose. What is important for any woman to develop— regardless of socioeconomic status or intellectual ability or eventual academic aspirations—is autonomy, competence in an area in which she can support herself, a positive image of herself, and knowledge of the options available to her.

NOTES

1. Charlotte Perkins Gilman, "Women and Education," from *The Man-Made World* (New York: The Charlton Co., 1911).

2. John Stuart Mill, *The Subjection of Women* (New York: Stokes Publ., 1911).

3. Mirra Komarovsky, *Women in the Modern World* (Boston: Little, Brown, 1953).

4. Eleanor Emmons Maccoby and Carol Nagy Jacklin, ed., *The Psychology of Sex Differences* (Stanford, Calif.: Stanford University Press, 1974), chapter 7, Power Relationships, esp. pp. 227–247. There is a vast body of literature on sex differences in aggression, and the entire argument is beyond the scope of this particular discussion. The reader is referred to Maccoby and Jacklin's excellent and exhaustive analysis of this research.

5. Elizabeth Fisher, "Children's Books: The Second Sex, Junior Division," in *And Jill Came Tumbling After: Sexism in American Education,* ed. Judith Stacey, Susan Bereaud, and Joan Daniels (New York: Dell Publishing Co., 1974), pp. 116–122.

6. Feminists on Children's Media, "A Feminist Look at Children's Books," in *Radical Feminism,* ed. Anne Koedt, Ellen Levine, and Anita Rapone (New York: Quadrangle, 1973), pp. 94–106.

7. List of notable books for children, *The Booklist,* vol. 72, American Library Assn. (no city), 1 April 1976.

8. *Daily Iowan,* 21 March 1975.

9. Janet Saltzman Chafetz, *Masculine/Feminine or Human?* (Itaska, Ill.: F. E. Peacock, 1974).

10. See, for example, Evelyn Carswell and Darrel L. Roubinek, *Open Sesame: A Primer in Open Education* (Santa Monica, Calif.: Goodyear Publishing Co., 1974).

11. Paul M. Kohn, "Relationships between Expectations of Teachers and Performance of Students (Pygmalion in the Classroom)," in *What Do You Expect? An Inquiry into Self-Fulfilling Prophecies,* ed. Paul M. Insel and Lenore F. Jacobson (Menlo Park, Calif.: Cummings Publishing Co., 1975), pp. 40–49.

12. Insel and Jacobson, 1975, op. cit., part 5.

13. Barbara Chasen, "Sex-Role Stereotyping and Prekindergarten Teachers," in Insel and Jacobson, 1975, op. cit., pp. 164–177.

14. Pauline S. Sears and David H. Feldman, "Teacher Interaction with Boys and with Girls," in Stacy, Bereaud, and Daniels, 1974, op. cit., pp. 147–158.

15. Patricia Cayo Sexton, *The Feminized Male: Classrooms, White Collars, and the Decline of Manliness* (New York: Random House, 1969).

16. Clarice Stasz Stoll, *Female and Male: Socialization, Social Roles, and Social Structure* (Dubuque, Iowa: Wm. C. Brown Co., 1974), p. 101.

17. Judith Hole and Ellen Levine, *Rebirth of Feminism* (New York: Quadrangle, 1971), p. 317, citing a 1969 study by the American Council of Education.

18. Robert Rosenthal and Lenore Jacobson, *Pygmalion in the Classroom: Teacher Expectations and Pupils' Intellectual Development* (New York: Holt, Rinehart and Winston, 1968).

19. Reported in Bette Levy, "Do Teachers Sell Girls Short?" *National Education Association Journal* (December 1972), pp. 27–29.

20. Chafetz, 1974, op. cit.

21. See, for instance, Barbara Grizutti Harrison, *Unlearning the Lie: Sexism in School* (New York: Liveright Publishing Corporation, 1973), p. 25.

22. Janice Law Trecker, "Women in U.S. History High-School Textbooks," *Social Education* (March 1971).

23. Chafetz, 1974, op. cit., p. 89. See also John Pietrofosa and Nancy Schlossberg, "Counselor Bias and the Female Occupational Role," in *Woman in a Man-Made World*, ed. Nona Glazer-Malbin and Helen Youngelson Waehrer (Chicago: Rand McNally, 1972), pp. 219–221.

24. Helen Astin, "Career Development of Girls During High School," *Journal of Consulting Psychiatry* 15 (1968), pp. 536–540.

25. Ronald G. Corwin and Alfred C. Clarke, "Social Change and Social Values," in *Explorations in Sociology and Counseling*, ed. Donald Hansen (Boston: Houghton Mifflin, 1969), p. 316.

26. Alice de Rivera, "On De-Segregating Stuvyesant High," in *Sisterhood Is Powerful*, ed. Robin Morgan (New York: Vintage, 1970), pp. 366–371.

27. E. L. McDill and J. Coleman, "High School Social Status, College Plans, and Interest in Academic Achievement: A Panel Analysis," *American Sociological Review* 28 (1963), pp. 905–919.

28. Pamela Roby, "Structural and Internalized Barriers to Women in Higher Education," in *Toward a Sociology of Women*, ed. Constantina Safilios-Rothschild (Lexington, Mass.: Xerox College Publishing, 1972), pp. 121–140.

29. B. F. Kirschner, "Introducing Students to Women's Place in Society," *American Journal of Sociology* 78 (1973), pp. 1051–1055.

30. Carole Ehrlich, "The Male Sociologist's Burden: The Place of Women in Marriage and Family Texts," *Journal of Marriage and Family* 33 (1971), pp. 421–431.

31. Z. S. Klapper, "The Impact of the Women's Liberation Movement on Child Development Books," *American Journal of Orthopsychiatry* 41 (1971), pp. 725–732.

32. Joan Acker, "Women and Social Stratification: A Case of Intellectual Sexism," *American Journal of Sociology* 78 (1973), pp. 174–183.

33. Jessie Bernard, "My Four Revolutions: An Autobiographical History of the ASA," *American Journal of Sociology* 78 (1973), pp. 11–29.

34. L. Schneider, "Our Failures Only Marry: Bryn Mawr and the Failure of Feminism," in *Woman in Sexist Society*, ed. Vivian Gornic and Barbara Moran (New York: Basic Books, 1971), pp. 419–436.

35. Mirra Komarovsky, "Cultural Contradictions and Sex Roles," *American Journal of Sociology* 52 (November 1946), pp. 184–189.

36. Matina Horner, "Fail: Bright Women," *Psychology Today* 3 (1969), pp. 36, 38, 62; Horner, "Toward an Understanding of Achievement-Related Conflicts in Women," *Journal of Social Issues* 28 (1972).

37. Adeline Levine and Janice Crumrine, "Women and the Fear of Success: A Problem of Replication," *American Journal of Sociology* 80 (January 1975), pp. 964–974.

38. Eleanor E. Maccoby, "Woman's Intellect," in *The Potential of Women*, ed. Seymour Farber and Roger H. L. Wilson (New York: McGraw-Hill Book Co., 1963), pp. 24–39.

39. Judith M. Bardwick and Elizabeth Douvan, "Ambivalence: The Socialization of Women," in Gornick and Moran, 1971, op. cit., pp. 225–241.

40. Ralph H. Turner, "Some Aspects of Women's Ambition," *American Journal of Sociology* 70 (1964), pp. 271–285.

41. K. Patricia Cross, "The Education of Women Today and Tomorrow," in *The American Woman: Who Will She Be?*, ed. Mary Louise McBee and Kathryn A. Blake (Beverly Hills, Calif.: Glencoe Press, 1974).

42. David Boroff, "The University of Michigan: Graduate Limbo for Women," in *The Professional Woman*, ed. Athena Theodore (Cambridge, Mass.: Schenckman, 1971), pp. 414–426, found that 40% of women graduate students at the University of Michigan were married. In both my graduate department and the department where I now teach, about half of the women sociology graduate students are married.

43. S. A. Husbands, "Women's Place in Higher Education," *School Review* 80 (1972), p. 261.

44. Saul D. Feldman, "Impediment or Stimulant? Marital Status and Graduate Education," *American Journal of Sociology* 78 (1973), pp. 220–232.

45. Boroff, 1960, op. cit.

46. Joseph L. McCarthy and Dale Wolfe, "Doctorates Granted to Women and Minority Group Members," *Science* 189 (September 1975), pp. 856–859.

47. P. J. Bickel, E. A. Hammel, and J. W. O'Connell, "Sex Bias in Graduate Admissions: Data from Berkeley," *Science* 187 (February 1975), pp. 398–404.

48. Barbara Deckard, *The Women's Movement: Political, Socioeconomic, and Psychological Issues* (New York: Harper and Row, 1975), citing John B. Parish, "Women in Professional Training," in *Monthly Labor Review* 97 (May 1974), p. 42. See also Roger M. Williams, "Law Schools: The Big Woman Boom," *Saturday Review World* (21 September 1974), pp. 51–54.

ADDITIONAL REFERENCES

1. Britton, Gwynneth E. "Sex Stereotyping and Career Roles." *What Do You Expect? An Inquiry into Self-Fulfilling Prophecies*. ed. Paul W. Insel and Lenore F. Jacobson. Menlo Park, Calif.: Cummings Publishing Co., 1975.

2. Couch, Carl. personal communication. 1974.

3. Dolon, Dan. "The Negative Image of Women in Children's Literature." *Elementary English*, April 1972, pp. 604–611.

4. Doty, C. N. and R. M. Haeflin. "A Descriptive Study of Thirty-Five Unmarried Graduate Women." *Journal of Marriage and Family* 26, 1964, pp. 91–95.

5. Howe, Florence. "The Education of Women." *Liberation Now!* ed. Deborah Babcox and Madeline Belkin. New York: Dell, 1971, pp. 293–305.

6. Howe, Florence. "Sexual Stereotypes Start Early." *Saturday Review World*, 16 October 1971, pp. 76–94.

7. Joffee, Carole. "Sex Role Socialization and the Nursery School: As the Twig is Bent," *Journal of Marriage and Family* 33, 1971, pp. 467–476.

8. Kohlberg, Lawrence. "A Cognitive-Developmental Analysis of Children's Sex-Role Concepts and Attitudes." *The Development of Sex Differences*. ed. Eleanor Maccoby. Stanford, Calif.: Stanford University Press, 1966.

9. Maccoby, Eleanor Emmons, and Carol Nagy Jacklin, eds. *The Psychology of Sex Differences*. Stanford, Calif.: Stanford University Press, 1974.

10. Roby, Pamela. "Women and American Higher Education." *Annals of the American Association of Political and Social Science* 404, November 1972, pp. 118–139.

11. Smith, M. "He Only Does It to Annoy." *Sex Differences and Discrimination in Education*. ed. S. Anderson. Worthington, Ohio: Charles A. Jones, 1972.

12. U'ren, Marjorie B. "The Image of Women in Textbooks." *Woman in Sexist Society*. ed. Vivian Gornick and Barbara Moran. New York: Basic Books, 1971, pp. 318–328.

13. Women on Words and Images. *Dick and Jane as Victims*. Princeton, N.J.: 1972.

4
WOMEN IN
THE ECONOMY

What is it that the many come to praise in the woman at work? They praise her docility. They praise her naiveté. They praise her availability. They praise her disappearance into the kitchen when they no longer need her.

—*Nancy Reeves*

LABOR FORCE PARTICIPATION

According to United States census reports, the labor force is all persons sixteen years old (or older) working for wages or actively looking for work. In 1972, the labor force consisted of 78.3 percent males and 43.3 percent females.[1] In 1940, only 27.4 percent of women sixteen and over were part of the labor force, but the proportion of women working has been increasing steadily since that time so that now the figure is 45 percent.[2]

The labor force has been expanding most rapidly in areas in which women already tend to be employed. In 1974, over one-third of all employed women worked in clerical jobs, and an additional 21 percent held service jobs. These proportions for women are increasing and show no evidence of stopping or reversing. The percentage of men in these two groups was 6.7 percent and 8.2 percent. Men tend to be concentrated in the category of blue-collar workers (45.9 percent), but are much more likely than women to be employed at the higher blue-collar levels of craftsman and foreman.[3]

From Nancy Reeves, *Womankind: Beyond the Stereotypes,* Chicago, Aldine, 1971, p. 61.

Despite their greater numbers in the occupational sphere, opportunities for women still are limited. Women are concentrated in an extremely small number of occupations. One-half of all working women were employed in only 21 of the 250 occupations listed by the Bureau of the Census, while half of all working men were employed in 65 of these occupations. Women also are more likely to be unemployed than men, as half of the unemployed are female, although only 40 percent of all employed persons are female.[4] These figures probably underrepresent unemployed women, as the statistics do not include the inactive unemployed who have given up looking for work, and who are more likely to be women, teenagers, and the elderly.[5]

Women form a marginal work force willing to take jobs that are part time, temporary, unstable, and poorly paid.[6] Within a "dual labor market," women constitute a "reserve army of the unemployed" who can be called upon to work when their labor is necessary or desirable, but who have no control over their situations because of their limited opportunities and lack of choice.[7]

Marital Status of Working Women
Of further interest is the change in marital composition of the population of working women. In 1940, only 36.4 percent of women in the labor force were married. That proportion has increased steadily so that by 1972, 63 percent of working women were married.[8] Not only are married women increasingly participating in the labor force, but women with children at home are also more likely to be found working. In 1950, only 11.9 percent of married women with children under six years of age were in the labor force, but by 1972 this proportion had risen to 30.1 percent. The female labor force has changed from one of primarily young, single women to one including older, married women whose children are grown, and most recently to one in which married women with young children at home are employed. Thus,

Table 4-1 Labor force participation rates of mothers and all women, selected years, 1954–74

Year	Mothers	All women
1974	45.7	45.2
1972	42.9	43.9
1970	42.0	43.3
1968	39.4	41.6
1966	35.8	38.9
1964	34.5	37.4
1962	32.9	36.6
1960	30.4	36.7
1958	29.5	36.0
1956	27.5	35.9
1954	25.6	33.7

Source: Table 11, p. 28, U.S. Dept. of Labor, Women's Bureau, *1975 Handbook on Women Workers*.

"... the female labor force has come to resemble much more closely the total female population."[9]

Wages

The utilization of women as a reserve labor force means that they can be paid the lower wages of part-time, temporary employees. Full-time, year-round working women in 1973 earned only 57 percent as much as full-time working men.[10] Far from finding the salary gap to be narrowing, the evidence is that the gap between men's and women's average salaries has been increasing. In 1955, full-time, year-round working women earned 64 percent of what men earned; in 1961, the proportion was 61 percent; by 1968, it was down to 58 percent, and in 1974 it was found to be 57 percent.[11] Some feel part of this could be attributed to intermittent work patterns and women leaving the work force, but Suter and Miller found that women who worked full-time every year since they left school still earned only 75 percent of the average salary of men.[12] The proportion varies with the type of work, but in no Department of Labor job classification do women earn more than two-thirds of what men earn in the same category. Even in the clerical worker category, which is predominantly female (78 percent in 1974), women workers in 1974 earned only 61 percent of the amount earned by men.[13] The largest proportion of men's income earned by women is in the "professional and technical" category, where women earned 64 percent of men's average earnings, and smallest in the sales category, where the proportion was 38 percent in 1974.[14]

Table 4-2 Median annual earnings of year-around full-time women workers by occupation, 1973

	Dollars	Percent of men's earnings
All occupations	6,340	57%
Professional & technical	9,090	64%
Managers & administrators	7,670	53%
Sales workers	4,650	38%
Clerical workers	6,470	61%
Craft workers	6,140	55%
Operatives	5,360	56%
Nonfarm laborers	4,960	61%
Service workers, except private household	4,590	58%

Source: Table 36, U.S. Dept. of Labor, Bureau of Labor Statistics, *U.S. Working Women, A Chartbook.* 1975.

In addition, women are much more likely to be poor and working for very low wages, as demonstrated by the fact that 45.7 percent of working women, but only 13.9 percent of working men, earned less than $5,000 in 1970. (On the other side of the coin, 1.1 percent of working women and 13.5 percent of working men earned over $15,000.[15]) Most of these workers are poorly paid because they are concentrated in the low paying job classifications, unable to rise to higher levels because of their limitations and/or because of their presumed temporary commitment to the job.

The President's Commission on the Status of Women in 1965 estimated that a young woman who marries and has a small family will spend an average of 23 years in the labor force. Over 90 percent of all women now do paid work at some time in their lives.[16] Marriage is not an alternative to a job for the 62 percent of poor adults who are women, because either they have no opportunity to marry or they are married and still must be in the labor force to survive. In 1970, of the six million working women who were poor, 4.3 million were service workers and 1.6 million private household workers. The vast majority of women workers are not unionized and have little hope of rising above the poverty level of income.[17]

Women earn much less than men with the same level of education; in 1970 a woman with four years of college earned less (at $8,156) than a man with only a high school education (at $9,567).[18] Women earn less than men even when work experience and hours of work are taken into account.[19]

The differences in salary are especially great for black women, who earn an even smaller proportion of men's salaries than do white women,[20] although there is some evidence that black women have made more rapid gains in economic advancement than white women since the civil rights activities of the 1960s.[21] Black women are also more like black men than white women are like white men in work patterns, status and income; but black women are still paid much less than black men with comparable education, work, hours, and experience.[22]

The Rich-Women Myth. Despite all the figures demonstrating the lower wages of women and their concentration in the poverty areas, the myth that women own most of the wealth of the country persists. In fact, Shirley Bernard, using Census Bureau data, shows that a larger proportion of men than of women hold assets of more than $60,000 in value; that more men individually hold stock than women; and that men more often than women leave estates of more than $60,000. As she concludes:

> *A study of the facts thoroughly discredits the clichés about women and their wealth. Not only are poor women poorer than poor men, but rich men are richer than rich women. . . . Men, not women, earn, own, and control most of the wealth of this country.*[23]

PARTICIPATION IN PROFESSIONS
Despite the greatly increased participation of women in the labor force, their involvement in the professions has increased little, if at all. While the proportion of women in the census category of "professional and

technical workers" has increased slightly in the last decades, this is largely explained by women's participation in the "female professions" such as nursing, social work, and elementary education. For other professional categories, increases in women's participation have not been apparent until very recently. Table 4-3 shows the proportion of all women workers in a few professions in the United States since 1910.

Table 4-3 Proportion of women workers in selected professions, 1910-60, U.S.

	1910	1920	1940	1960
Lawyers	1.0	1.4	2.4	3.5
College Presidents, Professors, Instructors	19.0	30.0	27.0	19.0
Doctors	6.0	5.0	4.6	6.8
Engineers	—	—	0.3	0.8
Dentists	3.1	3.2	1.5	2.1
Nurses	93.0	96.0	98.0	97.0
Social workers	52.0	62.0	67.0	57.0

Source: Adapted from Cynthia Fuchs Epstein, *Woman's Place: Options and Limits in Professional Careers*, Berkeley: University of California Press, 1971, p. 8, Table 1. Copyright © 1970 by The Regents of the University of California; reprinted by permission of the University of California Press.

Table 4-4, which shows more recent data, begins to reflect changes during the last few years, although none of these gains has been very large. Women as lawyers and judges have made the most dramatic increases, but their total proportion is still very small. Some headway has been made in college teaching. Women in 1974 accounted for 40 percent of the professional and technical workers, but not only was this a decrease from the peak of 45 percent in 1940,

Table 4-4 Occupational participation rates: women as a percent of the total employed workers, 1965-74

	1965	1970	1971	1972	1973	1974
Total employed (women as percentage of total labor force)	34.9	37.7	37.8	38.0	38.4	38.9
All professional	37.2	38.6	39.2	39.3	40.0	40.5
Lawyers & judges	3.7	3.8	3.9	3.8	5.8	7.0
Teachers at colleges and universities	23.8	24.1	25.6	28.0	27.1	30.9
Physicians	7.9	9.4	8.1	10.1	12.2	9.8
Accountants	19.2	23.3	21.3	21.7	21.6	23.7
Registered nurses	98.1	97.9	97.9	97.6	97.8	98.0
Social workers	59.6	66.5	65.7	58.6	60.8	61.3
Teachers of elementary school	86.9	84.2	84.9	85.1	84.5	84.3

Source: Stuart H. Garfinkle, "Occupations of Women and Black Workers, 1962-74," *Monthly Labor Review*, Vol. 98, No. 11, November 1975, U.S. Dept. of Labor, Bureau of Labor Statistics, Table 3.

but 70 percent of these workers were either nurses or non-college teachers.[24] As table 4-4 shows, these two professions have remained solidly female.

In addition to lack of improvement in job status, the relative income of women has not improved, partly because of their concentration at the lower income levels of each job classification and partly because of the tendency to pay women less money for the same work. From 1870 to 1950 women upgraded their occupational position more rapidly than men, but since 1950 male gains have been more rapid.[25]

Occupations were as sexually segregated in 1960 as in 1900. Male occupations have become rather more segregated (or resistant to female entry) while female occupations (such as teaching and social work) have become more open to males. It is the highly segregated jobs (e.g., clerical) which are growing fastest, which account for a large part of the overall increase in sex segregation.[26] While these findings have recently been challenged, it still remains a fact that the absolute degree of sexual segregation is "substantial."[27]

Women remain in the same relatively small number of sex-stereotyped occupations, with sex-typing of jobs remaining the norm and gaps in earnings increasing slightly. In 1974, 35 percent of all women workers were clerical workers, 18 percent service workers, 15 percent professional and technical workers and only 5 percent managers and administrators, with 2 percent in the crafts and kindred occupations. Women make up 98 percent of all private household workers, but only 18 percent of all managers and administrators.[28]

But the professions represent a special case of this more general issue of sex segregation in the labor market. A large part of the underutilization of women can be attributed to the sex-typing of work, since women still are considered appropriate only for a narrow range of occupations. Although various rationales have been developed to explain why certain jobs were for one sex or the other, ". . . by and large these rationales are used to exclude women from the prestigious male occupations . . ."[29] The idea that there are feminine and masculine professions is reflective of certain conceptions about the nature of women and men. "The female professions developed as extensions of the traditional role functions of the female in the family in tasks requiring nurturing, socializing, and helping."[30] However, despite this supposed principle, there is very little logical consistency about defining "helping" professions as women's work. Medicine can be seen as a prime example of the helping profession, and yet in this country medicine is overwhelmingly a male pursuit. It is only in the last two years that there have been indications that this pattern may change, as the number of women in professional schools is rising rapidly. Women now make up 17 percent of medical and 16 percent of law school students, and 11 percent of first year architecture students.[31]

Academe, Medicine, Law

Academe. What of those women who do enter law, medicine, academe? They still find themselves at the lower end of the salary and prestige scale within these professions. This "pyramid effect" holds for all the professions.[32] For instance, women are found to be a relatively small proportion of all full-time academic staff members.[33] They also tend to hold the lower status jobs, at smaller schools, at lower academic levels.[34] Women are less likely than men to be full professors, and are more likely to be in less prestigious research positions, rather than holding full academic appointments.[35] In 1971 women were found to be 9 percent of full professors, 16 percent of associate professors, 29 percent of assistant professors, and 35 percent of instructors.[36] In non-college teaching, women also are found concentrated at the bottom of the pyramid. Whereas women are the great preponderance (88 percent) of elementary school teachers, only 22 percent of elementary school principals are women and only 3.5 percent of high school principals are women.[37] High school teaching is about evenly divided between men and women, yet there is evidence that men in high school teaching are frustrated and regard it as a stepping stone to higher level administrative positions, resenting being paid "women's wages" for doing "women's work."[38] Men do tend to be successful at improving their status, as they are 94 percent of school superintendents.[39]

Medicine. In medicine, where women obviously represent only a very small proportion of the profession, even these few women tend to be channeled into certain areas and specializations. Women tend to specialize in pediatrics, psychiatry, and public health, and to avoid surgery.[40] However, despite the apparent "naturalness" of some of these distinctions, sex-typing in medicine is no more logically consistent than in other professions. Cynthia Fuchs Epstein points out that it is not necessarily stable hours of work or liberation from the entrepreneurial role which explains sex-typing within medicine, nor does it have to do with lesser demands or shorter residencies, as pediatrics, for example, is both demanding and requires a long residency. She argues that sex-typing reflects sex ranking, or that the first ranked jobs go to men, the first ranked sex.[41] Fields which are primarily women's fields, or which have a large female clientele, are considered less prestigious and are usually the least remunerative fields.[42] The story is the same for the health professions in general. Women are 71 percent of all health professionals, but three-quarters are concentrated in the categories of nurse, nurse's aide or orderly, and practical nurse. Women are only 10 percent of chiropractors, 4 percent of optometrists, 12 percent of pharmacists, 8 percent of podiatrists, and 5 percent of veterinarians, according to 1970 census data.[43]

Law. Women in law are a very small minority (3.5 percent), and are an even smaller minority of judges, and tend to be channeled into the less prestigious and less remunerative fields such as legal aid and matrimonial and family law, despite the fact that these practices may involve the most violent and brutal cases.[44] Women are found less often in tax, corporation, and real estate law. James White analyzed women lawyers in terms of such things as their ability, commitment, and turnover rates and found that none of these factors adequately accounted for the large income differentials between men and women lawyers, but rather explanations largely lay in discrimination against women lawyers by both employers and clients.[45]

Other Professions. Interestingly, women fare little better in the so-called female professions. Although two-thirds of social workers are women, men are twice as likely as women to hold administrative positions. Men are also more likely to hold national office in the National Association of Social Workers. In 1969 only 11 percent of deans and directors of accredited graduate schools of social work were women and the top executive of every major national social work organization (such as the Child Welfare League, the Family Service Association, or the National Urban League) was a man.[46] Women librarians fare somewhat better, in that there are more administrative opportunities in this field for women. However, while 85 percent of librarians are women, only about half of the head librarians are women, and men are more likely to be head librarians in larger colleges. Women head librarians are concentrated in colleges having less than 1500 students.[47] Large numbers of women are in the Civil Service, but again are concentrated at the lowest levels, with 47 percent in grades 1–6 and only 1.5 percent in grades 16 and above.[48] Many more examples could be cited for other professions.[49]

Sex-typing in Professions
Specialization in the professional sphere could not be explained by "natural" feminine and masculine characteristics, even if there clearly were such characteristics, since the sex-typing of professions changes over time and is different in different countries. The only qualities which the specifically "female" professions, or sub-specialties of professions, have in common is their lower status and their lesser remuneration.

"Affirmative action" and other such compensatory efforts are not going to change the sex-typing of professions. "Women's professions" tend to be specialized along the lines of expressiveness, person-orientation, and helping. This distinction helps to explain the so-called female professions like nursing and social work, but it is less successful in explaining why medicine is a male profession in the United States. In some societies, medicine is considered a "nurturant" profession; in the Soviet Union, for example, 75 percent of the doctors are women.[50]

The most "female" of the medical specialties, obstetrics and gynecology, are especially dominated by men in the U.S. When the delivery of babies by midwives was primitive and poorly paid, it was a female profession, but as it became "scientific," hospital-based, and expensive it became a male profession.

It is interesting that the "special qualities" which are said to qualify women so well for certain tasks are somewhat less useful for the more prestigious jobs. For instance, women are said to be particularly well-equipped for the detailed, fine, tedious work of assembling electronic components because of their fine finger dexterity and ability to withstand sustained work efforts. But, strangely, women are thought to have neither the manual dexterity nor the concentration nor the sustained energy required to perform surgery. Men, who are considered too clumsy to thread a needle, are supposed to be naturally superior at the careful work required by surgery.

Despite the apparent illogic of the sex-typing of professions, there *is* a certain consistency—if it pays well and is prestigious, it is man's work; if it pays poorly and has low status, it is woman's work. The amount of conflict with home roles also may be a basis for differentiation but it is not always applied when low-status, poorly paid work needs to be done. However, there is evidence that employers do think of possible role conflicts as a reason not to hire women. A survey of 1500 male executives found that they did not have complete confidence in a woman's ability to satisfy both family and job roles. In fact, they expected women to put their families above their jobs, and even felt that they *should*.[51] Others have discussed this role conflict for women as placing limits on their access to prestige professions.[52] The low rates of participation of women in the professions can be blamed only partly on discrimination in hiring, or even discrimination in admissions to professional and graduate schools. A great deal of the explanation lies in the woman's self-selection out of the rat-race for many reasons: because of the lack of support for her interest in a career; because of her own negative self evaluation and fear of success; because of her lack of role models and her belief that success is a remote if not impossible goal; because of the emphasis on family roles and goals; because of negative images and expectations about career women.[53]

RATIONALES FOR DISCRIMINATION

It is quite clear that women do not share equally in the fruits of labor force participation. The contention that women are paid equal pay when they perform equal work is one that can be neither verified nor refuted, since the idea of *equality* in performance is difficult, if not impossible, to measure. However, many persons who argue that women do not perform equally base their arguments on *facts* which are false and statements which are unverifiable. In 1970, the United States Department of Labor determined that more than $17 million in back pay was owed to 50,000 women who had received lesser wages for equal work. Despite the determination of the courts and the Department of Labor, employers have been known to state publicly that women should get lower pay because of their requirements for additional facilities, their greatly increased absenteeism rate, higher turnover rate, and the likelihood that they will quit to marry and raise a family.[54] Another common reason given for paying women less is that they don't really need to work, or that they don't need the money, and are working only for extras or luxuries. Explanations which have been given for discrimination in the work world center around two issues—that women don't need the money as much as men do, and that women workers are a poorer investment because of their higher costs.

Do Women Need to Work?

With regard to the need of women to work, research has indicated that a large proportion of women who work do so out of economic necessity. Twenty-three percent of working women are single, and another 19 percent are divorced, widowed, or separated. Of the remaining 58 percent of the female labor force who are married, 23 percent have husbands whose incomes are lower than $5,000.[55] In other words, the majority of women who work are either self-supporting or their work is necessary for the support of their families, to keep them above the poverty level. Families living in poverty are much more likely to be headed by women than men; 38.3 percent of families headed by women live in poverty, while only 8.3 percent of families headed by men do.[56] Another group of women may not work to keep their families above the poverty line, but nevertheless work out of necessity, rather than for "pin money" or frills. Many families require two salaries just to supply themselves with the basic necessities of life and a decent living. Thus, to state that women "don't need the money" is vastly to overestimate the number of working women who have husbands earning an adequate income. The fact is that the great majority of women work out of pressing economic need.

Do Female Employees Cost More?

The second issue deals with the cost of the woman worker to the employer. The argument has been that women workers are more expensive in terms of turnover, absenteeism, and special facilities. There is no evidence that women are less productive than men at non-physical work, although their jobs are routinely placed in lower job classifications and are paid less. There is also evidence that women are more productive than men under conditions requiring tedious, monotonous, boring production and assembly work. However, despite equal or better productivity, it is contended that women lose the advantage by being more expensive to the employer in terms of turnover and absenteeism. This belief has no basis in fact.

The United States Department of Labor has found that women workers have favorable records of attendance and labor turnover when compared with men employed at similar job levels and under similar circumstances. A public health survey study of days lost to illness or injury showed that women lost an average of 5.6 days per year to 5.3 days for men. Women are found to have slightly more illness episodes than men, but men's illness episodes last slightly longer, so that time out from work is very similar.[57] Even when differences in amount of sick leave do appear, the differences can be accounted for more by the type of work and level of pay than by the sex of the employee. When men and women at the same occupational levels, with similar salaries, are compared, the differences in length of sick leave disappear. "The highest average number of sick days occurred among those in the lowest salary levels—the levels where women workers are concentrated."[58]

As for turnover, it has been found that the rate of turnover per 100 employees was 5.2 for women and 4.4 for men. Of those, 2.6/100 were work quits for women, 2.2/100 for men, the rest for layoffs. This gap is very small and continues to narrow.[59] Further, Bureau of Labor statistics showed that men changed occupations more frequently than women, as 7 percent of the women and 10 percent of the men held different jobs from one year to the next. Some studies have revealed overall higher turnover rates for women, but where these are found, the higher rates for women can be explained by the lower level of job and shorter length of service. The Department of Labor conclusion was as follows:

> Meaningful comparisons of absenteeism and labor turnover of women amd men workers must take into consideration similar job levels as well as other factors such as age and length of service. Many of the critical generalities frequently voiced not only exaggerate overall differences but also compare dissimilar groups of men and women.[60]

Women do tend to leave work for reasons like childbearing and moving with their husbands, but men leave work approximately as often for different reasons, usually to improve their positions or leave intolerable ones. On the whole, absenteeism and turnover seem to have more to do with job level and job satisfaction, length of service, and age than with the sex of the employee.

Despite all rationales for differential pay and treatment, the "real" reasons lie in the sex-typing of jobs and sex segregation in the work world. The fact is that the economy is dependent on women as unpaid workers, and as a cheap reserve labor force. Women's work at home contributes immensely to the economy of the nation, although it is unpaid. Their paid work has been considered by many to be the element which keeps our economic system operating, for women leave the labor force when they are not needed, supplement it when they are, and replace men with cheaper labor when industry finds male labor becoming too costly. The large proportion of women who work part-time contributes to their attractiveness as employees, when the employer wishes to avoid work benefits accruing to full-time workers, and problems of seniority, pay increases and unionization.

The issues involved in labor force participation are in some ways very different for working-class women and for professional women. For working-class women, the most important issue is often survival, whereas equity and recognition of accomplishments are more important for professional women. It may seem at times that working-class women and professional women have nothing in common, especially when middle-class women discuss fulfillment, identity, and adding meaning to their lives through work. However, all women have a common interest in the issue of adequate remuneration for work performed, especially if the woman in question is responsible for her own support and possibly that of others. No woman benefits from the exploitation of her labor, or from creating an inexpensive reserve labor pool. Women do not benefit when the occupations they move into become defined as "women's work" and consequently are accorded lower status and less pay. Women of neither occupational level benefit from the fact that if they work they simply take on two workdays—one at work and one at home.[61]

No woman benefits from the general expectation that women have to prove themselves to be serious workers before they will be considered seriously, nor do they benefit from the assumptions that they will give up and quit without warning, or that they will be absent from work often. *All* women—regardless of occupation or income—suffer from the same kinds of limiting expectations and assumptions about their natures, and all suffer from the structural barriers erected to ensure their continued inequality. If it were at all realistic to expect to be supported forever, it might be acceptable to argue that many women would rather be in their homes, but the fact is that all women can expect to be part of the labor force, by choice or otherwise, for some part of their lives. Therefore, women of all occupational and income levels share the concern that they will be able to be economically independent, should the need arise.

HOW CAN WOMEN'S LACK OF SUCCESS BE EXPLAINED?

There is some basis in fact for the belief in the lesser career commitment of women. Given inadequate parental encouragement in early strivings for independence, the girl takes longer to become independent from her mother. Early childrearing experiences seem to fail to produce competence and self-confidence in girls, while prematurely pushing boys into independence and preoccupation with single-minded achievement. Either pattern may be unhealthy, but the feminine pattern is the one which produces a character least compatible with the cultural values of achievement and competitive striving.[62]

Not only are girls and women not trained and prepared for career commitment, but they actually are raised to avoid such commitment. Girls are taught to be flexible and open to a multitude of adult roles in order to facilitate adopting the role of wife and mother.[63] Not only is there a basic incompatibility between the childhood model of the supportive, sweet girl and the productive woman scientist or scholar,[64] but early family influences have their effect on cognitive style which results in small numbers of women developing the style of thinking necessary for scientific careers.[65]

There is also a considerable amount of evidence that the girl who later does show an interest in a career is likely to have been socialized somewhat differently from girls who are not career-oriented, or to have been presented with different role models or reference groups. These role models and reference groups are women who are able successfully to combine a home and an occupation, or who are deeply involved in their own careers and achievements. The work history of girls' mothers has been found to have a significant effect on girls' own career planning, in that the girl with a working mother as a role model is more likely to think in terms of her own future work.[66]

Internal Barriers
A woman may create her own barriers to opportunity, partly because she *does* have the alternative to choose not to compete, and is actually rewarded for *not* succeeding.[67] Cynthia Fuchs Epstein sums up the effects of early socialization:

> . . . because of their socialization, girls tend to accept definitions of what they might do; they do not aspire high. Even the smart ones, those who could become qualified, never are motivated sufficiently to attain the skills they would need later to become members of the professions. Although middle-class girls have a better chance to get a college education than lower-class girls, they seldom go on to get the necessary additional training necessary for working at jobs at the professional level. The socialization of the typical American woman affects the motivation even of the college educated woman and usually undercuts her career potential.[68]

Women tend to engage in "contingency planning," making plans for their own futures only on the contingency that a man lets them down by deserting them, dying, or failing to marry them. Contingency plans usually involve taking or preparing for some sort of job, but a woman ". . . usually is not expected to carve out a career or rise to a position of wealth and power. . . ."[69] Women may well be discriminated against in the job market, but more important is their own belief that they will not or need not succeed:

It is important to stress that although there are factors of reality which deflect women from choosing careers, the socialization process works on the woman in such a way that she often decides against a career without actually testing reality. Rather she anticipates consequences and accepts limitations or a defeat which may not be inevitable in her case.[70]

Images

Related to socialization practices and processes of sex-role learning is the learning of the appropriate image of woman in American society. Despite other factors in her environment, the girl cannot escape being subjected to an image of ideal femininity for our culture.

All societies define sex roles according to their images of the ideal man or woman. It cannot be too radical to assert that no human being is unaffected by these definitions, or can escape being measured according to these cultural images.

Although preferred female attributes and behavior vary over a considerable range, in most societies there is a core of preferred and imputed feminine attributes. In American society these include, among others, personal warmth and empathy, sensitivity and emotionalism, grace, charm, competence, dependence, and deference.[71]

The image of woman includes lack of aggressiveness, lack of personal involvement and egotism, lack of persistence, and lack of ambitious drive. Since these qualities are most desirable for professional and occupational success and intellectual achievement, this seems to mean that the role of ideal woman and the role of successful professional are mutually exclusive. Thus a woman either has to choose between them or to try to resolve the many conflicts and strains she will experience while trying to handle both. The choice of a career is difficult for *any* woman because the career woman "traditionally has been viewed as the antithesis of the feminine woman."[72]

Women are deprived of positive, supportive images relevant to career commitment: "At every turning the American woman is faced with a fresh decision of whether or not to work. And at each point of decision strong norms exist which weigh against going on."[73] A decision to give up a career for a home is often more approved than a decision to pursue a career. Images of women as a second sex, or as expressive rather than instrumental, fulfilled by home and children, and not needing outside achievement have been perpetuated by the mass media and by behavioral scientists alike. Many psychological views of normal adult women included ideas of dependency, submission, supportiveness and expressiveness. On the other side of the coin, Freudian psychoanalytic tradition tended to condemn ambitious or career-oriented women as "neurotic," "castrating," mannish and unfeminine.[74] Change will require changes in role models and psychiatric conceptions of the mentally healthy female.[75] However, today the normal adult woman is no longer expected to be dependent and submissive, and the career woman is no longer viewed as completely beyond the pale. In fact, such a term as "career women" seems out of date today in light of the current recognition of the importance of a number of satisfying roles for women. Women, today, seldom think in terms of career vs. marriage, but instead believe that they can successfully combine the two. As an increased number of women enter the labor force and the time spent on motherhood shortens, careers become more attractive to women, and old negative images of women with careers begin to decline. Recent polls and surveys show that a very large proportion of women feel career and job opportunities are of top importance to women, but at the same time very few women preferred to live alone.[76] My own research found the issues on which students were most liberal were those dealing with the acceptability of women breaking out of traditional roles, of pursuing traditionally "masculine" careers, and of the non-necessity of being wives and mothers for their fulfillment.[77] Ravenna Hilson found no evidence that career women were neurotic, dissatisfied, or less adjusted than women preferring their homes.[78] This old image of single-minded unfeminine career women simply does not fit today's facts.

External Barriers
Barriers to women are built into the occupational structure of American society because men set up job criteria which will automatically eliminate most women.[79] As far as "success" and "achievement" are concerned, a number of mechanisms work against accomplishments by women. For instance, researchers have discussed the effect of the family life cycle and bearing of children on women's careers. Aside from the mystique surrounding the maternal role is the fact of temporary removal from the labor force for childbearing and perhaps childrearing. An interruption of a person's career at this point may have very damaging effects on the eventual success of that career.[80]

The occupational system is geared to fit a man's reproductive cycle, not a woman's. A career-committed woman has to be aggressive in her work just at the time she is finding a husband and bearing and raising children.[81] If women are to be expected to carry out childbearing roles at this particular time of life, it might be expected that some changes could be made in occupations to accommodate women during this period, but there are no such mechanisms. Extensive day-care for children, flexible working schedules, part-time careers, and working at home are possible solutions which are rarely investigated. In fact, the necessity for such services as altered work schedules has been used to explain that women will never be as successful as men. Because their work schedules and life cycles *do* require special treatment and because they are willing to devote fewer hours and a less single-minded dedication to their professions, it is widely believed that women lack commitment to their professions.[82] As a result, the woman entering a profession often needs to prove that she is genuinely serious about pursuing a career.

Another important influence on the success of women in professions is their disadvantage in the sponsor or protege system. There is a tendency toward homogeneity and shared norms in the professions, so that anyone who is unlike the white male norm has some difficulty being accepted.[83] Jessie Bernard refers to the "stag effect" which involves being in the right professional communication channels or being excluded from informal male groups in various job and professional settings. Since much of what is considered important information and knowledge about the profession is passed on through these informal channels, being outside this interpersonal network may mean severe limitations on one's ability to grow and become socialized into the profession. Women, of course, are partly responsible for their own exclusion, and limit their own interaction with colleagues because of fear of rejection.

Women who do enter the competitive occupational setting often find that they encounter hostility and resentment, and if they survive the competition for positions of authority, may still encounter problems such as denial of status and denial of office information and shop talk. Promotions seem to come more slowly for women, thus making them older when they are ready for high-level jobs. At the highest levels, everyone is so well-qualified that choosing the best person may mean choosing the person who best "looks the part," so that credibility and self-confidence may count for more than competence. Men automatically may be favored when other things seem to be equal.[84] Outside of the professions there are built-in barriers in the legal protections and limitations imposed in work, and technical barriers in the form of machines designed for the size, strength, and hand shape of men.[85]

There are a number of ways to discriminate against women on the job. Devices to keep women from becoming too ambitious include ridicule, social rejection, bypassing them to promote men, and subtle forms of lowering expectations for women and not taking them seriously.[86]

Overt discrimination need not be practiced if employers assume there is a ceiling on a woman's financial worth.[87] Some believe that no matter how competent a woman is, she never is the equivalent of a brilliant man. Even when there is no intention to discriminate against women, cultural assumptions about the ability, commitment, and time a woman has to devote to her career limit the expectations of the employer about what she will achieve.

A final observation is offered by Patricia Albjerg Graham who points out that an institution may apply rules equally, but the rules themselves may favor one group over another. For example, the burden of business entertaining usually falls on the wife, even though both spouses may be professionally employed and both may benefit equally from the socializing.[88]

CONCLUSION

The question is, really, whether to choose to accept the reality which has been defined or whether to attempt to change that reality. The reality as it is known (and largely accepted) is that marriage and family are incompatible with a career for women; that women are entirely responsible for home and children; that women do not "need" to work and therefore deserve less in the way of job stability, status, and pay; that women workers are less capable than men workers and are worth less money; and that occupational achievement is incompatible with "femininity." None of these beliefs is "reality" any more than their opposites would be reality. They are simply social constructions, built upon physical sex differences and maintained over time by the force of tradition and by the functions that they serve in simplifying decisions about the division of labor.

The goal of a society should not be that every woman work, but that every person be given broader opportunities to choose, that a wider variety of alternatives be open to both sexes, and that advancement be equally possible for all. Rather than the changed reality causing working women to glut the labor market, it could incorporate new life styles which would call for modified work schedules, part-time work, and greater leisure time for men as well as women. The effect would be to include as many people as wish to work in the labor market, but with less pressure on any one person to devote his or her entire energies to breadwinning.

NOTES

1. U.S. Dept. of Commerce, *Statistical Abstract of the United States, 1972* (Washington, D.C.: Govt. Printing Office, 1972), table 348, p. 220.

2. Ibid., table 353, p. 222, and U.S. Dept. of Labor, Bureau of Labor Statistics, *U.S. Working Women: A Chartbook, Bulletin 1880* (1975).

3. Francine D. Blau, "Women in the Labor Force: An Overview," in *Women: A Feminist Perspective*, ed. Jo Freeman (Palo Alto, Calif.: Mayfield, 1975), pp. 211–226.

4. Anthony Costantino, "Women in the Economic Sphere: The Coming Struggle for Jobs," in *Women and Public Policy: A Humanistic Perspective*, ed. Mildred H. Lavin and Clara H. Oleson (Iowa City: Institute of Public Affairs, Univ. of Iowa, 1974), pp. 85–91.

5. Bette Gray, "Sex Bias and Cyclical Unemployment," in *Woman in a Man-Made*

World, ed. Nona Glazer-Malbin and Helen Youngelson Waehrer (Chicago: Rand McNally, 1972).

6. Costantino, op. cit.; Blau, op. cit.

7. Blau, op. cit., p. 220.

8. *Statistical Abstract,* op. cit., table 353, p. 222.

9. Blau, op. cit., p. 223.

10. *U.S. Working Women: A Chartbook,* op. cit.

11. U.S. Dept. of Labor, Women's Bureau, figures; see also Blau, op. cit; Costantino, op. cit.; L.E. Suter and H.P. Miller, "Income Difference Between Men and Career Women," *American Journal of Sociology* 78 (1973), pp. 962–975.

12. Suter and Miller, op. cit.

13. *U.S. Working Women: A Chartbook,* op. cit., chart 36.

14. Ibid.

15. U.S. Dept. of Labor, Women's Bureau, figures.

16. U.S. Department of Labor, *Manpower Report of the President* (Washington, D.C.: Govt. Printing Office, March 1973).

17. Kathleen Shortridge, "Working Poor Women," in Freeman, op. cit., pp. 242–253.

18. U.S. Dept. of Labor, Women's Bureau, *Fact Sheet on the Earnings Gap, 1970* (Washington, D.C.: Govt. Printing Office, 1970).

19. Donald Treiman and Kermit Terrell, "Sex and the Process of Status Attainment: A Comparison of Working Women and Men," *American Sociological Review* 40 (April 1975), pp. 174–200.

20. Esther Peterson, "Working Women," in *The Woman in America,* ed. R. J. Lifton (Boston: Houghton Mifflin, 1965); U.S. Dept. of Commerce, *Statistical Abstract of the United States, 1971* (Washington, D.C.: Govt. Printing Office, 1971).

21. Alan L. Sorkin, "Education, Occupation, and Income of Nonwhite Women," *Journal of Negro Education* 41 (Fall 1972), pp. 343–351.

22. Treiman and Terrell, op. cit.; see also Sally Hillsman Baker and Bernard Levenson, "Job Opportunities of Black and White Working-class Women," *Social Problems* 22 (April 1975), pp. 510–532.

23. Shirley Bernard, "Women's Economic Status: Some Cliches and Some Facts," in Freeman, op. cit.

24. Barbara Sinclair Deckard, *The Women's Movement: Political, Socioeconomic, and Psychological Issues* (New York: Harper and Row, 1975).

25. Sorkin, op. cit.

26. Edward Gross, "Plus ca Change . . . ? The Sexual Structure of Occupations Over Time," in *The Professional Woman,* ed. Athena Theodore (Cambridge, Mass.: Schenkman Publishing Co., 1971), pp. 39–51.

27. Gregory Williams, "A Research Note on Trends in Occupational Differentiation by Sex," *Social Problems* 22 (April 1975), pp. 543–547.

28. *U.S. Working Women: A Chartbook,* op. cit., chart 9.

29. Cynthia Fuchs Epstein, *Woman's Place: Options and Limits in Professional Careers* (Berkeley: University of California Press, 1971). Copyright © 1970 by The Regents of the University of California reprinted by permission of the University of California Press.

30. Theodore, op. cit., p. 57. See also Margaret Adams, "The Compassion Trap," in *Woman in Sexist Society,* ed. Vivian Gornick and Barbara Moran (New York: Basic Books, 1971), pp. 555–575.

31. Deckard, op. cit., p. 139.

32. Ibid.

33. Ruth E. Eckert and John E. Stecklein, "Academic Women," in Theodore, op. cit., pp. 346–354, report women are 22% of full-time academic staff members; Patricia Albjerg Graham, "Women in Academe," in Theodore, op. cit., pp. 720–740, reports 18%; Jessie Bernard, *Academic Women* (University Park: Penn. State Univ., 1964), p. 30, reported 19.5%.

34. See Bernard, 1964, op. cit., p. 63; Eckert and Stecklein, op. cit.; Graham, op.

cit.; Ann E. Davis, "Women as a Minority Group in Higher Academics," in Theodore, op. cit., pp. 587–598.

35. U.S. Dept. of Labor, Women's Bureau, figures; Davis, op. cit.

36. Judith Hole and Ellen Levine, *Rebirth of Feminism* (New York: Quadrangle, 1971), p. 317.

37. U.S. Dept. of Labor, Women's Bureau, figures.

38. Harmon Ziegler, "Male and Female: Differing Perceptions of the Teaching Experience," in Theodore, op. cit., pp. 74–92.

39. Patricia A. Schmuck, "Deterrents to Women's Careers in School Management," *Sex Roles* 1 (December 1975), pp. 339–353.

40. Epstein, 1971, op. cit., p. 155; J. Kosa and R. E. Coker, Jr., "The Female Physician in Public Health: Conflict and Reconciliation of the Sex and Professional Roles," *Sociology and Social Research* 49 (1965), pp. 294–306. See also Deckard, op. cit.; Lillian Kaufman Cartwright, "Conscious Factors Entering into Decisions of Women to Study Medicine," *Journal of Social Issues* 28 (1972), pp. 201–216; Carol Lopate, "Marriage and Medicine," in Theodore, op. cit., pp. 494–515.

41. Epstein, 1971, op. cit., p. 162.

42. Ibid., p. 164.

43. U.S. Bureau of the Census, Decennial Census, 1970.

44. Epstein, 1971, op. cit., p. 161.

45. James J. White, "Women in the Law," in Theodore, op. cit., pp. 647–659.

46. Aaron Rosenblatt, Eileen M. Turner, Adalene R. Patterson, and Clare K. Rollesson, "Predominance of Male Authors in Social Work Publications," *Social Casework* 51 (1970), pp. 421–430.

47. W. C. Blankenship, "Head Librarians: How Many Men? How Many Women?" in Theodore, op. cit., pp. 93–102.

48. U.S. Civil Service Commission, Manpower Statistics, *Study of Women in the Federal Government, 1968* (Washington, D.C.: Govt. Printing Office, 1968).

49. See, for instance: E. W. Bock, "The Female Clergy: A Case of Professional Marginality," *American Journal of Sociology* 72 (1967), pp. 531–540; Cynthia Fuchs Epstein, "Encountering the Male Establishment: Sex-Status Limits on Women's Careers in the Professions," *American Journal of Sociology* 75 (1970), pp. 965–983; Epstein, "Women Lawyers and Their Profession: Inconsistency of Social Controls and Their Consequences for Professional Performance," in Theodore, op. cit., pp. 669–684; H. Etzkowitz, "The Male Sister: Sexual Separation of Labor in Society," *Journal of Marriage and Family* 33 (1971), pp. 431–435; S. F. Fava, "The Status of Women in Professional Sociology," *American Sociological Review* 25 (1960), pp. 271–276; John Kosa, "Women and Medicine in a Changing World," in Theodore, op. cit., pp. 709–719; E. L. Linn, "Women Dentists: Career and Family," *Social Problems* 18 (1971), pp. 393–404; Lopate, op. cit.; L. Nochlin, "Why Are There No Great Women Artists?" in Gornick and Moran, op. cit., pp. 344–367; Stanley S. Robin, "The Female in Engineering," in Theodore, op. cit., pp. 397–413; Alice Rossi, "Who Wants Women in the Scientific Profession?" in *Women in the Scientific Professions,* ed. Jacqueline A. Mattfield and Carol G. Van Aken (Cambridge: M.I.T. Press, 1965); Rossi, "Women in Science: Why So Few?" in Theodore, op. cit., pp. 612–628; Martha S. White, "Women in the Professions: Psychological and Social Barriers to Women in Science," in Freeman, op. cit., pp. 227–237; R. S. Willett, "Working in 'A Man's World': The Woman Executive," in Gornick and Moran, op. cit.; Patricia A. Yokopenic, Linda Brookover Bourque, and Donna Brogan, "Professional Communication Networks: A Case Study of Women in the American Public Health Association," *Social Problems* 22 (April 1975), pp. 493–509.

50. Epstein, 1971, op. cit., pp. 154–159.

51. Benson Rosen, Thomas H. Jerdee, and Thomas L. Pretswich, "Dual-Career Marital Adjustment: Potential Effects of Discriminatory Managerial Attitudes," *Journal of Marriage and Family* 37 (August 1975), pp. 565–572.

52. R. L. Coser and G. Rokoff, "Women in the Occupational World: Social Disruption

and Conflict," *Social Problems* 18 (1971), pp. 535–554; Margaret M. Poloma and T. Neal Garland, "The Myth of the Egalitarian Family: Familial Roles and the Professionally Employed Wife," in Theodore, op. cit., pp. 741–761.

53. For an interesting recent article on how women participate in their own lack of success in academic settings, see Lora Liss, "Why Academic Women Do Not Revolt: Implications for Affirmative Action," *Sex Roles* 1 (September 1975), pp. 209–223.

54. Caroline Bird, *Born Female: The High Cost of Keeping Women Down*, rev. ed. (Pocket Books, 1971), p. 34.

55. Blau, op. cit.

56. Bernard, 1975, op. cit.

57. U.S. Dept. of Labor, "Facts About Woman's Absenteeism and Labor Turnover," in Glazer-Malbin and Waehrer, op. cit., pp. 265–271.

58. Ibid., p. 270.

59. Ibid.

60. Ibid., p. 271.

61. See Olga Domanski, "Pages from a Shop Diary," in *Liberation Now!*, ed. Deborah Babcox and Madeline Belkin (New York: Dell, 1971), pp. 88–94; Jean Tepperman, "Two Jobs: Women Who Work in Factories," in *Sisterhood Is Powerful*, ed. Robin Morgan (New York: Vintage, 1970).

62. Lois Wladis Hoffman, "Early Childhood Experiences and Women's Achievement Motives," *Journal of Social Issues* 28 (1972), pp. 129–155.

63. Shirley S. Angrist, "Measuring Women's Career Commitment," *Sociological Focus on Sex Roles* 5 (Winter 1971–72), pp. 30–39.

64. Rossi, in Mattfeld and Van Aken, op. cit.

65. Rossi, in Theodore, op. cit.

66. E. M. Almquist and S. S. Angrist, "Career Salience and Atypicality of Occupational Choice Among College Women," *Journal of Marriage and Family* 32 (1970), pp. 242–250.

67. Cynthia Fuchs Epstein and Wm. J. Goode, "The Position of Women Today," in Epstein and Goode, op. cit.

68. Epstein, *Woman's Place*, 1971, op. cit., p. 51.

69. Ibid., p. 75.

70. Ibid., p. 76.

71. Ibid., p. 20.

72. Ibid., p. 23.

73. Ibid., p. 27.

74. Helene Deutsch, *The Psychology of Women*, Vol. 1 (New York: Grune and Stratton, 1944).

75. K. Keniston and E. Keniston, "An American Anachronism: The Image of Women and Work," *The American Scholar* 33 (1964), pp. 355–375.

76. *Chicago Tribune*, 9 February 1975.

77. Carol A. Whitehurst, "Developing a Scale of Attitudes Toward Women's Roles," 25 June 1975, unpublished; see also Karen Oppenheim Mason, John L. Czajka, and Sara Arber, "Change in U.S. Women's Sex-Role Attitudes, 1964–1974," *American Sociological Review* 41 (August 1976), pp. 573–596.

78. Ravenna Helson, "The Changing Image of the Career Woman," *Journal of Social Issues* 28 (1972).

79. Bernard, 1971, op. cit., p. 109.

80. Rossi, in Theodore, op. cit.

81. Bird, op. cit., p. 48.

82. There is some substantiation for the idea that women are less career committed than men. See, for instance, Bernard, 1964, op. cit.

83. Epstein, *Woman's Place*, 1971, op. cit., p. 167.

84. See Bernard, 1964, op. cit., p. 111.

85. Robert Gubbels, "The Supply and Demand for Women Workers," in Glazer-Malbin and Waehrer, op. cit.

86. Alice Rossi, "Job Discrimination and What Women Can Do About It," in Babcox and Belkin, op. cit., pp. 67–75.

87. Bird, op. cit., p. 63.

88. Graham, op. cit. See also Lynda Lytle Holmstrom, *The Two-Career Family* (Cambridge, Mass.: Schenkman Publishing Co., 1972).

ADDITIONAL REFERENCES

1. Bell, Carolyn Shaw. "Age, Sex, Marriage and Jobs." *Public Interest* 30, Winter 1973, pp. 76–87, for a review of data on working and unemployed women.

2. Bernard, Jessie. *Women and the Public Interest.* Chicago/New York: Aldine-Atherton, 1971, pp. 124–125.

3. Epstein, Cynthia Fuchs. "Women and the Professions." *The Other Half.* ed. Epstein and Wm. L. Goode. Englewood Cliffs, N.J.: Spectrum, 1971, p. 122.

4. Knudsen, Dean. "The Declining Status of Women: Popular Myths and the Failure of Functionalist Thought." *Social Forces* 48, December 1969, pp. 183–193.

5. Komarovsky, Mirra. "Cultural Contradictions and Sex Roles." *American Journal of Sociology* 52, November 1946, pp. 184–189.

6. Oppenheimer, Valerie Kincaid. "Demographic Influence on Female Employment and the Status of Women." *American Journal of Sociology* 78, 1973, pp. 946–962.

7. Reeves, Nancy. *Womankind: Beyond the Stereotypes.* Chicago: Aldine, 1971, p. 61.

8. Suelzle, Marijean. "Women in Labor." *Trans-Action* 8. November–December 1970, pp. 50–58.

5
LEGISLATION AND THE POLITICAL INSTITUTION

Little girls do not dream of growing up to be governor.

—*Peggy Lamson*

The status of women in society is often reflected in laws which regulate behavior and participation in public life. Not all discriminatory laws are overtly oppressive, but where laws discriminate arbitrarily on the basis of sex, there is oppression. Laws can be changed only by legislators and others in power and are most likely to be changed by those people they most benefit. When a particular group (such as women or minorities) lacks representation in legislative bodies, it may be assumed that that group cannot speak for itself and that its interests are not being made known. Such groups traditionally have lacked their own power base, being obliged to rely on the good graces of those who are in power. Since the changes which would most benefit the powerless are not always the first priority of those who are already in power, legislative change to aid the powerless is usually very slow in coming. This chapter will deal with legislation concerning women, the present legal status of women, and the political power of women with regard to voting and holding public office.

From Peggy Lamson, *Few Are Chosen*, New York: Houghton Mifflin, 1968, p. xxii.

LEGISLATION AFTER THE NINETEENTH AMENDMENT

After the 1920 ratification of the Nineteenth Amendment, granting women's suffrage, the legislative status of women in the United States changed very little until the 1960s. The Women's Bureau of the Department of Labor began collecting data and publishing statistical reports on the status of women after the passage of the Nineteenth Amendment, but it was not until 1964 that the differential treatment of women and men documented in these reports became a legal issue.

Title VII and EEOC

In 1964 Title VII of the Civil Rights Act was enacted prohibiting discrimination in employment on the basis of sex. Originally almost as a joke, the word "sex" had been added to the list of characteristics which could not be considered valid criteria for employment. It was felt that to require that Title VII include sex as a basis for nondiscrimination would make the bill difficult to pass.[1] Liberals also believed that it would be harder to enforce and would detract from the benefits of the bill to racial groups.

The ban against sex discrimination was submitted as an amendment by Rules Committee Chairman Howard W. Smith of Virginia and adopted with strong Southern support, despite opposition by the U.S. Department of Labor and the objection by House Judiciary Committee Chairman Emanuel Celler that it was "illogical, ill-timed, ill-placed, and improper." It is widely believed that Southern support for the amendment was an attempt to hamstring the agency which would administer the title by taking resources and energy away from its handling of race-discrimination cases.[2]

However, despite dire predictions about the effect of the sex-discrimination ban on the Act, the bill passed and it became illegal to discriminate on the basis of sex as well as race, religion, and national origin. Shortly thereafter, the Equal Employment Opportunities Commission (EEOC) was created to enforce the new civil rights law. Forty percent of EEOC complaints involved sex discrimination, outnumbering those in any other category.[3]

Important legislation of the 1960s included the Fair Labor Standards Act, amended by the Equal Pay Act in 1963, and Executive Order 11246 (1965) forbidding all Federal contractors from discriminating in employment because of race, religion, color, or national origin. Two years later this was amended by Executive Order 11375 which added a prohibition against discrimination by sex, and also required "affirmative action" by asking employers to describe in detail the specific steps they planned to take toward eliminating discrimination on the basis of sex.[4] Since that time, "affirmative action" guidelines have called upon employers to "recruit women actively for the full range of positions the organization can offer and to set goals and timetables for hiring and promoting women for assignment at levels in which they are under-represented."[5]

Legislation, once enacted, has not been ignored by women's groups. In 1970, WEAL (Women's Equity Action League) officially charged the University of Maryland with sex discrimination. This action was the first complaint under the amended Executive Order 11246. Since then many other suits and class actions have been filed against many colleges and universities. Title IX of the Education Amendments Act of 1972 prohibits sex discrimination in educational programs receiving federal money, along with the Equal Employment Opportunity Act (EEOA) of 1972 which eliminated an old exemption for educational institutions. Title IX prohibits sex discrimination in schools at all levels and affects admissions, scholarships, and courses, as well as hiring, salaries, promotions, and course assignments of teachers. The EEOA specifically deals with equal recruitment, promotion, and salaries for female and male faculty members.

ERA, Pro and Con

Of all the important legislation for and about women in recent years, probably the most important and far reaching is the Equal Rights Amendment (ERA). The ERA has been introduced into Congress every year since 1923, but not until March 1972 did it pass both houses of Congress. Since that time 34 of the 38 states necessary have ratified the Amendment. ERA simply states, "Equality under the law shall not be denied or abridged by the United States or any state on account of sex."[6] It makes laws that arbitrarily differentiate between the sexes unconstitutional, which means only that laws can be designed neither for the protection nor the limitation of either sex. Groups of all kinds began to back the ERA in 1969 and 1970, usually on the basis of favoring simple equality. It was argued that ERA would eliminate the necessity for all sorts of further legislation.

Opponents have argued that such a law is not possible because women and men are different and live different lives. The strongest opposition comes from those who see the ERA as threatening the family and the home. They feel it will force a woman to assume an independent status whether she wants to or not, while assaulting the man's role as breadwinner and head of household. Others are concerned over the implications for women of loss of alimony, loss of protective legislation, loss of nearly automatic custody of children, and loss of draft exemption.

According to Senate Report 92-689, the Equal Rights Amendment "will require that the federal government and all state and local governments treat each person, male and female, as an individual. It will not require that any level of government establish quotas for men or for women in any of its activities; rather it simply will prohibit discrimination on the basis of a person's sex. The amendment will apply only to government action; it will not affect private action or the purely social relationships between men and women."[7] Backers of ERA feel that this amendment is necessary because the Supreme Court has not interpreted the Fourteenth Amendment, which gives the right to equal protection and due process of law to all persons, to apply to women. Other legislation, such as the 1964 Civil Rights Act, only applies to employment and private industry. And although a number of states have already adopted their own equal rights legislation, a single amendment would insure that all states do so and within a specified period of time.

Opponents of ERA argue that this particular piece of legislation is not necessary and will cause untold legal and social problems. A major emphasis of the opposition is the feeling that it would interfere with marriage and the family and destroy the foundation of family life, because it would take away a wife's legal right to support, force women to work, abolish child support, and remove a woman's right to custody of her children. Other charges are that ERA will remove protective legislation for women, allow women to be drafted and serve in combat, allow homosexual marriage, abolish laws pertaining to rape, prostitution, adultery, and obscenity, and allow shared public restrooms and sleeping facilities.[8]

Common Cause has prepared a pamphlet to present questions and answers on this Amendment. Their research indicates that ERA "will not deprive women of alimony, custody of children, or child support; it will only require that men be eligible for alimony under the same conditions of women . . . ; that the welfare of the child be the criterion in awarding custody in contested cases . . . ; and that mothers be responsible for child support *within their means.*"[9] ERA also does not mean that a woman will be deprived of her right to choose to be a housewife and housewives need not fear that husbands will not be required to support them and their children. Protective laws which discriminate by sex will be invalidated, but where the laws are meaningful, they would be expanded to include both men and women. Women would be drafted if there were a military draft for men, and would serve both in and out of combat zones. However, women would also become eligible on the same basis as men for military benefits, services, preferences, and exemptions. ERA would have no effect on rape laws, because laws applying only to women in rape cases are not based on *arbitrary* sex discriminations. Other backers suggest that laws against sex crimes would be rewritten to apply equally to men and women. Men and women would not be expected to share sleeping quarters and bathrooms because of the constitutional right of privacy. The amendment may or may not legalize homosexual marriage, but state laws could possibly prohibit homosexual marriages as long as the laws applied equally to both sexes.

Although most of the opposition seems to come from groups and individuals whose primary concern is the disintegration of the family,[10] there is also concern on the part of working women that ERA will hurt working women by eliminating protective legislation rather than extending these laws to men.[11] At this point, it is not clear because the equal rights laws have not been adequately tested. A number of legislators and researchers feel that the passage of the ERA would eliminate the need for other special legislation and that this is its most important feature. Although recent court decisions have demonstrated the principle of equality under the law for men and women (for instance, the *Frontiero* v. *Richardson* decision of 1973 allowing a female member of the uniformed services to claim her student husband as a dependent), political action groups continue to work for legislative change in particular areas. In other words, without the all-inclusive legislation of the ERA, specific changes still are needed in abortion and rape laws, credit discrimination rules, insurance laws, social security benefits, and in ending discrimination in housing, pensions, and inheritance.

Recent Change

The legal status of women has changed and improved significantly in recent years. In 1975, the Supreme Court ruled that awarding Social Security benefits to the children of a deceased worker could not be differentiated on the basis of the sex of the wage earner. However, Social Security still does not apply to women who work in their own homes, and it discriminates against people who drop out of the labor force for extended periods of time, as women often do when raising their children. Another positive change has come with the 1975 Credit Opportunity Act which puts an end to discrimination in loans, mortgages, and charge accounts on the basis of sex or marital status. Many other advances have been made by the passage of historic legislation and by landmark Supreme Court decisions, but each of these only serves to underscore the fact that a great deal of such piecemeal legislation will be required without the more general Equal Rights Amendment. The ERA is expected to change this pattern of scattered gains.

LEGAL STATUS OF WOMEN

As recently as 1966, in Texas, a woman was found not liable to pay back a loan because a married woman did not have the capacity to enter into a binding contract on her own. Although it has been some time since women were legally considered the property of males, remnants of this attitude remain, for instance, in laws which regard the wife's domicile legally that of her husband. This residence requirement means that a woman must vote and run for office from the domicile of her husband, regardless of her own residence. In some cases, a woman who marries a man from another state must pay out-of-state college tuition in her own state, as her legal residence is considered that of her husband.[12] Legal restrictions on the rights of married women to enter into contracts remain in several states.

On the other side of the coin, men are considered more responsible for the support of families, and therefore are liable to creditors and are legally responsible for alimony and for child support. Only men can be prosecuted for crimes such as statutory rape and for the use of "vulgar" language in front of women and children.[13] However, while a man is seldom convicted of murder in the case of his wife's adultery, the belief in this "unwritten law" is not applied to women in the case of the husband's adultery.

Protective Legislation
One of the most important areas of difference in laws regarding women and men is the area of "protective laws." Protective legislation restricts the working hours and working conditions of women. Although such legislation discriminates in favor of women in some ways (by providing for rest periods, lighter duties, better working conditions), it has been argued that this protection is uneven, and actually has had the effect of saving the premium overtime and better jobs for men.[14] Women are "saved" from working long hours or late at night, which precludes them from earning time-and-a-half, or from working at certain lucrative night jobs. These protective laws are unevenly applied as women are not "protected" from working as night nurses or as cleaning women and entertainers. On the other hand, women are not guaranteed the right to get their jobs back after maternity leave[15] nor are they given any special consideration regarding maternity leave. It seems that protective legislation was not meant to protect the woman's physical well-being, but was meant to protect the continuance of the human race.[16] Or, as Eastman put it, a woman's status has been that of servant to man and to the state, and women were protected to keep the home fires burning and to raise the next generation.[17]

Gains in Legal Rights
Gains in legal rights are being made in almost all areas. Women are now entitled to serve on juries in federal and state courts, a right not granted in some states until the 1960s. In Louisiana, until 1975, women were required to register their willingness to serve on juries rather than to be selected from lists of voters as men were.[18] Another gain was made when the Supreme Court ruled against a required four months' maternity leave for public school teachers in Cleveland.[19] Another 1975 court decision ruled that states must set the same age of majority for both sexes.[20] Other laws that discriminate against women are being struck down by individual states, such as prostitution laws which

provide only for the prosecution of women prostitutes rather than their customers, and rape laws which require women victims to have corroborating witnesses and to expose their private lives to the court.[21]

States are moving in the direction of greater legal equality between the sexes. For example, the legislative priorities of the Iowa Commission on the Status of Women include the following: provision for child care; laws concerning inheritance; credit and insurance discrimination; pension and survivor benefits; changes in Social Security laws and Social Security benefits for homemakers; inclusion of the contributions of women in school curricula; and legislation against housing discrimination. Other target areas include laws regarding maternity leave, rape (changing requirements both for evidence and testimony), and decriminalization of female "sex" crimes such as prostitution. Another major area of reform is in juvenile justice, with the intention of removing incorrigibility and promiscuity as chargeable offenses, since only females are incarcerated for this sort of "crime."[22] Finally, with regard to dissolution of marriage, there are proposals which would require consideration of the real economic value of the contributions of the dependent spouse as a homemaker, and would consider the cost of educating and training the dependent spouse.[23]

Despite the advances which have been made and which continue to be made in the legal status of women, a number of issues are as yet unresolved. Organizations such as NOW (National Organization for Women) and WEAL (Women's Equity Action League) can be expected to continue to work for further legislation. One important problem with the new legislation has been with its interpretation and implementation. For example, Title VII of the 1964 Civil Rights Act prohibits discrimination in employment on the basis of sex, but employers are exempted when sex is a "bona fide occupational qualification." Although Equal Employment Opportunity Commission guidelines are now rather specific on what could be considered a bona fide qualification, this has been taken to include disqualifying a woman from employment because she had small children.[24] These problems are being worked out, but discrimination against both women and men remains.

POLITICAL POWER
Voting
Women in 1972 represented 53.1 percent of all persons of voting age in the United States.[25] Women are a slightly smaller percentage of registered voters (52.6 percent in 1972) and are slightly less likely than men to vote if registered. In 1972, 64.1 percent of all male registered voters actually voted, while 62.0 percent of registered women cast their vote.[26] However, because of their greater numbers in the population, the absolute number of women actually casting votes

outnumbered the men. Therefore, while women are slightly less likely than men to register, and slightly less likely than men to vote if registered, they still cast the majority of votes in national elections.

Much has been made of the fact that women register and vote in smaller proportions than men, but the differences between them have been steadily narrowing since women were granted the vote, and the difference is now only about two percentage points. The difference in voting patterns is much greater in certain regions of the country, particularly in areas where women have been confined to a more tradi-tional role. In the South, only 48.3 percent of males voted in 1970, but an even smaller 41.6 percent of women voted.[27] Despite the fact that the differences are so small as to seem substantially insignificant, data have also been collected on reasons for not registering and voting. However, no difference between women and men has been found in reasons given or in interest indicated. The differences between men and women in giving "not interested" as a reason for not registering is less than two percentage points (43.6 percent for women, 42.0 per-cent for men). The difference on "dislikes politics" is 6.7 percent for women, 8.6 percent for men. (In other words, *more* men gave as a reason for not registering, and also for not voting, that they disliked politics.) The reason given by women substantially more often than men was that they were unable to register or unable to go to the polls, presumably because of home responsibilities and lack of transportation.[28]

In Public Office
These figures show clearly that women potentially command a great deal of political power and that they are no more indifferent to the use of their vote than male voters. However, despite the potential, it is obvious that women do not use this power of the vote to elect them-selves to positions of leadership. Nothing is more obvious than the fact that women do not hold elective or appointive political offices pro-portionate to their numbers in American society. Not only has there never been a woman U.S. President, Vice President, or Supreme Court Justice, there has never been more than one or two female Senators at a time. Women usually represent only about 2 percent of Congress. The proportion of women in public office has remained constant at about 2.5 percent.[29] Between 1917 and 1971, 69 women served in the House of Representatives and 10 in the Senate. Until 1975, when Carla Anderson Hills was appointed Secretary of Housing and Urban Devel-opment, there had been only two women cabinet members (Frances Perkins, Secretary of Labor in 1933 and Oveta Culp Hobby, Secretary of Health, Education and Welfare in 1953), about a dozen ambassa-dors, and a very few top judges.[30]

Until the election of 1974, there had been only three women governors in the history of the United States and all three had succeeded husbands who had died or who were unable to run for another term. In 1974, Ella T. Grasso was the first woman to be elected governor of a state (Connecticut) in her own right. The same year saw the election of the first woman mayor of a large city, Janet Gray Hayes of San Jose, California.[31] In North Carolina, Susie Sharp was the first woman elected Chief Justice of a state supreme court. Eighteen women, a record number, were elected to the House of Representatives. In state legislatures, 587 women were elected, a clear increase over the 470 serving before the election of 1974.

The accomplishments of women in the elective arena simply serve to underscore the fact of their usual absence. While the fact that women attained the vote hardly meant that they had political power, neither did the small increase in office-holding signal any real change in power. Women are still, by and large, excluded from major power centers and women as a group lack any resources other than sheer numbers to trade in for political influence. Even women who are elected are relatively powerless, as they tend to serve short terms and are rarely appointed or elected to serve on or head important committees.[32] Opportunities for women in politics have been very restricted in the past and even now show only slight evidence of change. According to Jeane Kirkpatrick, there will be no great rise in the number of women politicians in the United States without a dramatic change in America's social, educational, and economic priorities. A gradual inclusion of women in power processes is the more likely trend.[33]

One explanation for the lack of women in politics is that they express their social and political interests in ways different from office-holding. One popular belief holds that some political wives do influence the opinions of their political husbands, thus exerting political influence. However, this can hardly be considered an equivalent to holding formal power.

> . . . women have been rather adequately socialized to influence those who had power (men) through a range of subtle, devious and indirect techniques and many of them became quite skilled in operating backstage, in the underground, diplomatically, tactfully so that the powerful men would never discern that they were being influenced. Throughout history women have been the very influential wives, mistresses, daughters, and sisters of powerful presidents, dictators, ministers, generals, or governors. They have probably often been responsible for significant decisions made by these men.[34]

On the other hand, Kirsten Amundsen argues that personal influence or "bedroom power" is really a myth, and that such power may help the woman's personal situation, while not changing her social one.[35]

As Volunteer Workers

Women do have the potential to influence political processes in another setting than the bedroom, however, since women make up the vast majority of political volunteer workers. Martin Gruberg and others have found that the political campaigning efforts of women have been responsible for a number of political victories and elections of important candidates.[36] Janet Saltzman Chafetz has pointed out that without the voluntary political participation of women political parties could scarcely function. Although the women rarely have any access to power, partly because of their lack of wealth or independent position, "without their extensive *volunteer* services . . . the machinery of politics would fall apart."[37] Chafetz adds that women do all the dull, routine tasks which must be done to keep things running, while men are freed for "important" things like deciding strategy and policy. Amundsen also points out that women's lack of representation in political office cannot be explained by their abstinence from party politics and campaign activities, because they are so obviously interested and important as volunteers. She adds that the norm in politics is to encourage volunteering for women but to give a cold shoulder to ambitions beyond that.[38] In an unpublished study of a volunteer campaign worker in a successful senatorial campaign, it was discovered that women were relegated to certain types of duties, namely that women held the jobs closest to housekeeping and wifely duties. In this campaign, only women did the office work (typing, answering phones, sending mail) while men tended to be sent to work in the field. The writer, who was also a campaign worker, noted that potential sponsors often would not deal with women as true representatives of the candidate although they were willing to deal with men. However, the author observed that in the office women were treated "like secretaries," but when in the field they were listened to and treated as people rather than just women. Apparently someone who had "proven herself" to this extent was taken seriously as a qualified experienced campaigner.[39]

Doris Gold has pointed out that volunteering may make women feel associated with power, but it does not represent real power. Volunteering in political campaigns by women is actively encouraged, although not to train women for future positions of leadership. Rather, volunteerism is encouraged because it is innocuous and uncontentious and deflects people from seeking real power by channeling them into less threatening directions.[40] A recent survey showed that only 18 percent of the top presidential campaign jobs are held by women, indicating that they are not given very frequent opportunities to learn the political ins and outs.[41]

Not all women believe that volunteer work is unimportant; some feel it may be the best way to train to be a candidate yourself. In an Iowa City panel discussion sponsored by Women's Political Caucus, four women who had been active campaign managers, county chair-persons, and party committee members seemed to agree that for the potential candidate there was no better training ground.[42] Women's Political Caucus itself is an organization devoted to gaining political power for women and influencing the political process. It goes beyond endorsing candidates and working in campaigns as it also raises money and supports women in running for political office. Women involved in this group tend to feel that their goals will be reached when women as a group enjoy greater political power.

Voting Patterns

A large part of the reason women's suffrage was so long in becoming law was that at one time the power of women as a group was feared. William Chafe has pointed out that once it was realized that women were not voting as a bloc, concessions were no longer made to them.[43] Suffrage therefore failed to change the status of women and seemed to create no opportunity to develop a positive sense of collective con-sciousness. As a result, women tended to follow the lead of their hus-bands and fathers in voting.[44] Although women are using their ballots in ever-higher numbers, the voting pattern remains much as it was during the 1920s. According to Carol Andreas, "the legalization of suffrage for women has not noticeably affected their participation as equals at all levels of government."[45] Neither has it meant that women were likely to vote for a certain kind of issue or candidate. Basically, women vote very much as men do, and most married women tend to vote like their husbands. They do not vote as a bloc and traditionally have not tended to support women candidates.[46] There is some evi-dence that in certain European countries women tend to vote more moderately than men, voting more often for "central" than for ex-treme "left" or "right-wing" parties.[47] Women are actually more likely to be "conservative" on such issues as war and military spending (in the sense of opposing such spending), but more "liberal" on social welfare and issues such as poverty, racism, and capital punishment.[48] There is no evidence that women vote for the "sexy" candidate or that they are distinctly different from men in any other aspect of voting. Finally, although women have not traditionally supported women candidates in the United States, Elina Haavio-Manila found in her Finnish study that women were much more likely than men to vote for women candidates.[49] There are indications in the last few years that this pattern may be developing in the U.S. as well.

And so we return to our original question: women potentially have a great deal of power because of their numbers and their vote, so why do they fail to use it? Amundsen suggests creating woman power in politics involves actually using the vote, making demands known to the elected representatives, and getting their own people into power.[50] The first step does not seem to be problematic, and women are beginning to make some progress with the second. It is the third—electing women to positions of power—that seems most elusive. The barriers to achieving this are of particular interest.

Barriers to Obtaining Formal Power

The power to affect political orientations is perhaps the most crucial form of power in a democracy, and without it present inequities are not likely to change.[51] Legislation for women cannot be passed without either sympathetic male office holders who are influenced by female lobbyists and interest groups, or women elected themselves. As we have seen, very few women run for office or are elected; until this situation changes, there is little reason to believe that there will be any particular recognition of female concerns. Given the importance of legislation, laws, and political decisions to all of our lives, why do so few women become interested in political office? The answer seems to lie in the areas of socialization, cultural definitions of the woman's role, and outright prejudice and discrimination.

Congresswoman Patsy Mink has said, "Politics may be the last and most difficult area of 'breakthrough' for women . . . the barriers to women in politics are mainly based on custom which no court can eradicate."[52] The "custom" argument can be expanded into that of the nature and definition of the female role in our society. Andreas has pointed out that traditionally women have held "modest" roles, not suitable for the rigors of political campaigning and office holding.[53] Still more restrictive are the norms regarding "woman's place" and the traditional and romantic sex-role ideologies which state that politics belong to men. Haavio-Manila has reported from Finland that subjects of both sexes found it far more important for men than for women to take an interest in politics. She found that sex roles did not influence the *way* women voted, but "the influence of sex role ideologies could be seen primarily in voting *for* women."[54] In other words, women's roles did not keep women from voting, but they did keep women from running and from being elected for office. The feeling that it simply is not *right* for a woman to enter such a cutthroat and aggressive world as politics is still a very effective barrier to political participation by women. The reciprocal expectations of what women should do—namely to be mothers, homemakers, supporters and suppliers of gentleness and glamour—are equally large barriers to women entering politics. The very qualities which create a "feminine" woman are exactly those which render her unsuited for political activity:

Sweetness, passivity and helplessness may be appealing qualities in a variety of situations, but the political is not one of them. A woman whose self-concept is entirely what sexist ideology would have it be is not likely to make independent judgments, to voice her opinions, or to take political responsibilities. . . . It is not too much to say then, that to the ex-

tent it has taken hold the effect of sexist ideology has been to disarm the American woman politically and also to deprive American democracy of the politically informed and intelligent contribution of more than half of its citizenry.[55]

It is fairly clear that adhering to a traditional feminine role is antithetical to achieving in the political arena because of cultural definitions, expectations and attitudes about what women *should* do, and what they should *not* do. These same role definitions also include the notion of deference to males, and the belief that men *should* be dominant and in leadership positions. These attitudes are held by women and men alike, and largely explain a woman's lack of interest in politics as a career.

Early Differences
Internal barriers to achievement in politics may also be a result of early childhood socialization and continuing socialization throughout life. Most girls have been trained to believe that women are unable and unwilling to wield power. They are socialized to be women first and citizens second. Throughout the process of socialization, girls are given systematically less leadership training and training for aggression and achievement. Girls (and boys) are raised to believe that men are better suited emotionally for politics than women. In a recent poll, a majority of people (63 percent) agreed that this was true.[56]

Studies of early sex differences in political interests and activities have found that girls and boys in elementary school differ in political-related interests. This pattern is much stronger in adulthood, when political interest and concern are found to be substantially higher for men. Actual political knowledge is found to be greater for boys in virtually all political socialization research, and this greater knowledge continues into adulthood. Amundsen notes that women seem to learn less and feel less competent in dealing with politics. Studies support the notion of lower levels of political efficacy in women,[57] suggesting that a sense of efficacy develops with participation itself. Apparently political aspirations are not encouraged in the same way for girls.[58]

While it is clear that adult men engage more often than adult women in political activity and express greater political awareness and concern, it is not entirely clear that this is a result of being socialized to believe that politics is not a woman's "place." It has been suggested that women may even purposely cultivate a lack of knowledge about politics (and such other areas as sports) during the dating years so as to give their dates and boyfriends topics in which they could easily be more knowledgeable.[59] For these and other reasons, women tend to develop fears and inhibitions, greater self doubts, and lesser leadership qualities. A person with great doubts and few positive leadership qualities is not likely to become a political candidate. And besides having less confidence and far fewer skills and techniques (of speaking, decision-making, leading, wielding power), a woman also finds that she has no support for a decision to enter such an area. Not only does she have lower (almost non-existent) positive pressures to run for office or be politically active, but she also has greater pressures *not* to do so.

Despite sex differences in the political activity of adults, A. M. Orum and his colleagues found no significant differences between boys and girls in political affect (interest), participation, or discussion. The researchers felt that adult differences either were a result of situational and structural factors impinging on the adult, or that childhood sex differences in political socialization were disappearing. However, the researchers found a sex difference in political knowledge (although not in interest or participation), which they suggested could be an indication of anticipatory socialization. Boys, then, were anticipating entering the public world of work, and girls the private world of the home, expressing this in lesser knowledge of politics. In sum, the effects of socialization were confined mainly to the cognitive (knowledge) realm.[60]

Problems of Women in Political Office

The presence of internalized barriers, acquired through socialization experiences and later role expectations, are at least matched by external and structural barriers. Not only the woman's perceptions of the ideal female role, but the nature of the family and her actual family role requirements often preclude taking an active part in political life, especially if she has children. These role requirements mean that even if a woman does enter the political arena, the decision is usually delayed until the children are older, which may mean that she loses time, experience, and the power base necessary to become politically effective.[61]

Another common problem of female legislators is that they encounter a system of male bonding, "old boy" informal networks, and socializing in settings which exclude females. It is commonly noted that much of political decision making goes on in the informal setting of the locker room, golf course, or bar, from which women are normally excluded. As a result, women have very limited influence and more often introduce legislation on "feminine" or "soft" subjects such as health, housing and education and consumer affairs and are rarely appointed to the "hard" (and important) "masculine" committees, dealing with defense, international affairs, ways and means and the like.[62]

Most people still find it very hard to imagine a woman for President, and one survey found that most people polled did not expect a woman President in less than about fifty years.[63] Another poll reported that more of the electorate was willing to vote for a qualified black man (67 percent) than for a qualified woman of any race (54 percent).[64] The trends may be changing, as voters have become more and more disillusioned with traditional politics and politicians, but women as yet have not begun to make a dent in the political system.

Jeane Kirkpatrick surveyed 46 female state legislators and reported that they were less upwardly striving, less "on the take," more committed to a moralist conception of politics, and more interested in the pursuit of the public good than men.[65] Lamson, who studied ten women holding public office, tended to agree with others that women in public office are more attentive to details, more genuinely concerned with people, and more conscientious than men. She also found that they took themselves and their work seriously, were realists but were not cynical, sometimes were more cautious and defensive, and on the whole, were quite ambitious and determined.[66] This bodes well for female politicians at the present time, but does not mean that politics will completely change its nature with an infusion of new blood. Although people tend to believe that women are more idealistic, peace-loving, humanitarian, and gentle, the actions of women in the past cannot be taken as an indication of how they would react if finally given equal access to power. There is no particular reason to believe that more women in legislative bodies will create a more humane and just society.[67]

CONCLUSION

Some women are interested in learning the skills and techniques of exerting power, and are beginning to search for their own power bases and coalitions. These women have started to learn about power and influence through their own efforts through Women's Political Caucus, Women's Lobby, and other special interest groups. A large part of the impetus for change came from the women's movement itself. Women's high participation in the 1972 National Conventions also supplied many women with some skills and knowledge as well as a taste for political action and power. With the greatly expanded interest in legislation concerning women in recent years and the small but steady gains being made in political office, it appears that women may attain some chance to participate in major decision-making processes in American society. Even if this does not mean a more humane and peace-loving nation in the long run, in the short run it is important to encourage women to assume political positions for two reasons. The first deals with simple equity, as no other group is so glaringly under-represented in positions of power. Second, there is strong sentiment that the best people are not attracted to politics, and a larger base from which to choose elected representatives is needed.

The talent, energy, ability, and enthusiasm of more than half of our population is wasted when women are not considered for political candidacy. Maurine Neuberger, a former United States Senator from

Oregon, felt that there were hardships, frustrations, and heartaches involved in a political campaign, but that participating in the governing of the country was ample reward.[68]

NOTES

1. Caroline Bird, *Born Female: The High Cost of Keeping Women Down*, rev. ed. (New York: Pocket Books, 1971), chapter 1.

2. Alice Rossi, "Job Discrimination and What Women Can Do About It," in *Liberation Now!*, ed. Deborah Babcox and Madeline Belkin (New York: Dell, 1971), p. 71.

3. Carol Andreas, *Sex and Caste in America* (Englewood Cliffs, N.J.: Prentice-Hall, 1971); Joreen, "The 51 Percent Minority Group: A Statistical Essay," in *Sisterhood Is Powerful*, ed. Robin Morgan (New York: Vintage, 1970).

4. Robin Dorr, "Education and Women's Rights: What the Law Now Says," *American Education* 8 (December 1972), pp. 4–10.

5. Ibid., p. 9.

6. Common Cause, "Equality of Rights . . . Shall Not Be Abridged . . . On Account of Sex," *Questions and answers on the proposed 27th Amendment to the Constitution, now before the States for ratification* (Washington, D.C.: Common Cause, n.d.).

7. Ibid.

8. Lisa Cronin Wohl, "Phyllis Schlafly: The Sweetheart of the Silent Majority," *Ms.* 11 (March 1974), pp. 54–57, 85–89. See also Denise Derkacs, "ERA—What Does It Mean?" *Quad City Times*, Davenport-Bettendorf, Iowa, 28 February 1975.

9. Common Cause, op. cit.

10. Wohl, op. cit.

11. Joan Jordan, "Comment: Working Women and the Equal Rights Amendment," *Trans-Action* 8 (November-December 1970), pp. 16–22.

12. Janet Saltzman Chafetz, *Masculine/Feminine or Human?* (Itasca, Ill.: F. E. Peacock, 1974), p. 140.

13. Leo Kanowitz, *Women and the Law: The Unfinished Revolution* (Albuquerque: University of New Mexico Press, 1969).

14. Bird, op. cit., p. 168. For an extensive discussion of the effects of protective legislation, see Karen De Crow, *Sexist Justice* (New York: Vintage, 1974).

15. Bird, op. cit.

16. Diane B. Schulder, "Does the Law Oppress Women?" in Morgan, op. cit.

17. Mary Eastman, "Feminism and the Law," in *Women: A Feminist Perspective*, ed. Jo Freeman (Palo Alto, Calif.: Mayfield, 1975), pp. 325–334.

18. Ibid. See also Lesley Oelsner, "Legal Status of Women Has Changed Drastically," New York Times News Service, *Cedar Rapids Gazette*, 30 March 1975.

19. Eastman, op. cit.

20. Anonymous, "Sex-Equality Backers Win in High Court," AP News Service, *Riverside* (Calif.) *Press*, 15 April 1975.

21. Oelsner, op. cit.

22. Iowa Commission on the Status of Women, *IoWoman*, Vol. IV, No. 2 (Des Moines, Iowa: May 1974).

23. *IoWomen*, Vol. V, No. 1 (January 1975).

24. Brian Richard Boylan, *The Legal Rights of Women* (New York: Award Books, 1971). See also De Crow, op. cit., chapter 5.

25. U.S. Bureau of the Census, *Current Population Reports*, Series P-20, No. 244, "Voter Participation in November 1972 (advance statistics)" (Washington, D.C.: Govt. Printing Office, 1973).

26. Ibid.

27. U.S. Bureau of the Census, *Current Population Reports*, Series P-20, No. 228, "Voting and Registration in the Election of November 1970" (Washington, D.C.: Govt. Printing Office, 1971).

28. U.S. Bureau of the Census, *Current Population Reports, Series P-20, No. 253,* "Voting and registration in the Election of November 1973" (Washington, D.C.: Govt. Printing Office, 1973).

29. Peggy Lamson, *Few Are Chosen* (New York: Houghton-Mifflin, 1968), p. xxii.

30. Clarice Stasz Stoll, *Female and Male: Socialization, Social Roles, and Social Structure* (Dubuque, Iowa: Wm. C. Brown Co., 1974), p. 196.

31. For this purpose, a large city was defined as one with a population of over 500,000.

32. Chafetz, op. cit.

33. Jeane Kirkpatrick, *Political Woman* (New York: Basic Books, 1974).

34. Constantina Safilios-Rothschild, *Women and Social Policy* (Englewood Cliffs, N.J.: Prentice-Hall, 1974).

35. Kirsten Amundsen, *The Silenced Majority* (Englewood Cliffs, N.J.: Prentice-Hall, 1971).

36. Martin Gruberg, *Women in American Politics* (Oshkosh, Wis.: Academia Press, 1968).

37. Chafetz, op. cit.

38. Amundsen, op. cit., p. 85.

39. Connie Goeb, "Women in Politics: The Campaign of Berkley Bedell," unpublished, December 1974.

40. Doris Gold, "Women and Voluntarism," in *Woman in Sexist Society,* ed. Vivian Gornick and Barbara Moran (New York: Basic Books, 1971), pp. 384–401.

41. Anonymous, "Find Women's Roles in Campaigns Small," AP News Service, *Des Moines* (Iowa) *Register,* 26 January 1976, reporting a survey by the Washington Institute for Women in Politics.

42. Jen Madsen, Gertrude MacQueen, Linda Weeks, and Joanne Soper, "The Role of Women in Campaigns," panel discussion, Johnson County (Iowa) Women's Political Caucus, 13 February 1975.

43. William Chafe, *The American Woman: Her Changing Social, Economic, and Political Role, 1920–1970* (London: Oxford University Press, 1972).

44. Ibid.

45. Andreas, op. cit., p. 105.

46. Safilios-Rothschild, op. cit., p. 147.

47. Ibid.

48. Gloria Steinem, "Women Voters Can't Be Trusted," *Ms.,* July 1972, pp. 47–51, 131.

49. Elina Haavio-Manila, "Sex Roles in Politics," in *Toward A Sociology of Women,* ed. Constantina Safilios-Rothschild (Lexington, Mass.: Xerox College Publishing, 1972), pp. 154–172.

50. Amundsen, op. cit., p. 65.

51. Ibid., p. 100.

52. Patsy Mink, "Women: The New Figure in American Politics," in *The American Woman: Who Will She Be?,* ed. Mary Louise McBee and Kathryn A. Blake (Beverly Hills, Calif.: Glencoe, 1974), pp. 107–118.

53. Andreas, op. cit.

54. Ibid., p. 171.

55. Amundsen, op. cit., p. 133.

56. Virginia Slims poll, cited in Safilios-Rothschild, 1974, op. cit., p. 144.

57. Campbell et al., *The American Voter* (New York: John Wiley and Sons, 1960); Lester W. Milbrath, *Political Participation* (Chicago: Rand McNally, 1965).

58. Lamson, op. cit., p. xxvi.

59. This idea was suggested to me by Lynn Munro Nollenberger.

60. A. M. Orum et al., "Sex, Socialization, and Politics," *American Sociology Review* 39 (1974).

61. See Safilios-Rothschild, 1974, op. cit. for further discussion of this issue.

62. Frieda Gehlen, "Women in Congress," *Trans-Action* 6 (October 1969), pp. 36–40.

63. Virginia Slims Poll, cited in Safilios-Rothschild, 1974, op. cit.
64. Reported in Amundsen, op. cit., p. 67.
65. Kirkpatrick, op. cit.
66. Lamson, op. cit.
67. See a similar argument in Safilios-Rothschild, 1974, op. cit.
68. Lamson, op. cit., p. xii.

ADDITIONAL REFERENCES

1. Campbell, Angua; Philip E. Converse; Warren E. Miller; and Donald E. Stokes *The American Voter.* New York: John Wiley and Sons, 1960.

2. Greenstein, Fred I. *Children and Politics.* New Haven, Conn.: Yale University Press, 1965.

3. Hess, Robert D., and Judith V. Torney. *The Development of Political Attitudes in Children.* Chicago: Aldine, 1967.

4. Hyman, Herbert. *Political Socialization.* Glencoe, Ill.: Free Press, 1959.

5. Iglitzen, Lynne B. "Political Education and Sexual Liberation." *Politics and Society* 2, Winter 1972, pp. 241–254. Iglitzen suggests this is changing with women's liberation.

6. Jaquette, Jane S. *Women in Politics.* New York: Wiley-Interscience, 1975, for more extensive analysis of the issues discussed in this chapter; also Tolchin, Susan and Martin. *Clout: Womanpower and Politics.* New York: Coward, McCann and Geoghegan, 1975.

7. Lane, Robert E. *Political Life: Why People Get Involved in Politics.* Glencoe, Ill.: Free Press, 1959.

8. Lazarsfeld, Paul F.; Bernard Berelson; and Hazel Gaudet. *The People's Choice.* New York: Columbia University Press, 1968.

9. Lipset, Seymour Martin. *Political Man.* New York: Doubleday, 1960.

10. Merelman, Richard M. *Political Socialization and Educational Climates: A Study of Two School Districts.* New York: Holt, Rinehart and Winston, 1971.

11. Milbrath, Lester W. *Political Participation.* Chicago: Rand McNally, 1965.

12. Orum, A. M.; R. S. Cohen; S. Grasmuch; and A. Orum. "Sex, Socialization, and Politics." *American Sociological Review* 39, 1974, pp. 197–210.

6
PROFILE OF AMERICAN VALUES

"Who was that lady I saw you with last night?"
"That was no lady, that was my wife."

There is no neat or completely consistent and integrated value system in American society. Our value system is characterized by diversity and change. While there have been a number of ways of viewing dominant values of American society, it is clear that no *single* value system exists. American values have been discussed by historians, anthropologists, sociologists, and scholars of American culture looking for recurrent themes in literature and descriptive studies of American life. Most have found emphases on such things as achievement, mastery of the self and environment, happiness, and equality of opportunity.[1] We will discuss the bases for some of these views.

HISTORICAL APPROACH
In 1831, Alexis de Tocqueville spent a year observing American society, which prompted him to write the two-volume work *Democracy in America*.[2] In his book De Tocqueville found the democratic ideal to be the common bond among Americans. The American character that de Tocqueville described is practical and oriented toward progress and change, contemptuous of tradition and contemplation, preferring the pursuit of worldly welfare, the indefinite improvement of humankind,

and the active life. Americans also place a high value on independence, freedom, and individualism.[3]

He described the American woman as having a masculine education and many of the qualities and attitudes of men, but as losing her independence at marriage. Marriage requires self-abnegation, the constant sacrifice of her pleasure to her duties, the voluntary surrender of her own will, and circumscription within a narrow circle of domestic interests and duties. De Tocqueville did not see this as oppressive, however, because he felt that both men and women regard their own pursuits as important and of equal value. He described the situation as one of extreme dependence and narrow sphere for women, and thus of social inferiority, but of moral and intellectual equality. He concluded that this situation is welcomed by women, who perceive that their only road to domestic happiness lies in devotion to husband and home.[4]

Geoffrey Gorer concluded that Americans place early emphasis on the individual's independence and self-reliance, although he noted that this begins earlier and is more likely to be emphasized for boys than for girls. Gorer found that the predominant American philosophy is pragmatism, that the American man dominates his material objects, is superior to, rather than identified with his "things," and imposes his will on the universe. Women, Gorer added, are not oriented toward domination of things but are oriented toward people.[5]

According to Gorer, Americans feel that the object of life is to be a success, but since success is not clearly defined, the social value of one's efforts has come to be measured in dollars. Despite a fundamental belief in equality, one's ultimate worth seems dependent on success and achievement. Differences in success are attributed to individual ability, industry, and luck.[6]

Robin Williams, recognizing that there is no completely consistent value structure in American society, nevertheless was able to suggest broad value orientations. He included activity and work, achievement and success, concern with moral codes and ethics, humanitarian mores, efficiency and practicality, progress, material comfort, equality if deserved, freedom, external conformity, rationality, nationalism, democracy, individual personality, and group-superiority.[7]

Florence Kluckhohn has noted that there are both dominant cultural orientations and alternate (or substitute) cultural orientations, and these alternative value systems can be based on such distinctions as class, race, sex, or age. Her description of the dominant American value system is one in which activism, futurism, individualism, and achievement guide the actions of a majority of Americans.[8]

Williams and Talcott Parsons also have both explicitly recognized the diversity of values and the deviant patterns of value orientations in any society. Total endorsement of all the values suggested is not possible, and exceptions may vary by position in the social structure.

Parsons' most important exception to the general adherence to the dominant value system is the case of women, to which we will return.

WOMEN IN AMERICAN SOCIETY

The value systems of women in American society can be viewed in a number of ways. Women may live by an alternative standard of values which is adapted to their own needs and is fulfilling to them. Another possibility is that women live according to a modified version of the dominant standard, or a "shadow system." Another variation is the double standard, or "separate but equal" value standard for women. Finally, women may live not by a variation of the dominant standard, but by directly opposed values.

Kluckhohn suggests that women live by standards which are directly opposite to those which men adopt. She argues that the behavior expected of women in the wife-mother role is based on values which are markedly different from dominant American values, best expressed in the occupational role.[9] While the dominant value system requires a "doing" personality type, the woman fits better the "being in becoming" type, which emphasizes what the person is rather than what she can accomplish. Men are seen as active, *doing,* so women can take care of the leisure, recreational, and cultural pursuits.[10] Kluckhohn also argues that women are not future-oriented, but are expected to be oriented to tradition rather than change.[11] While men look ahead, plan, and save, women are limited to vicarious participation in future planning.[12]

Kluckhohn goes on to say that women in traditional roles are more collaterally than individualistically related to others. Men's relationships tend to be individualistic, while women are expected to be more dedicated to group goals, especially in the family group. Thus, there seems to be a dominant role and dominant values which support it (the male role and values), and a variant or alternative role and values which support it (the female role and values). These roles are not complementary, as they constitute separate systems where men represent normal society and women stand outside. Under this cultural double standard, certain expectations seem to be polar opposites for the two sexes.

The qualities, values and roles expected of women are required to supply the necessary balance to the male emphasis on achievement and aggression. The fact that women are not supposed to live up to the dominant cultural values means that the alternative (so-called "feminine") values are necessary to maintain and reinforce an ongoing system of male values and the institutions based on these values. It is only through women assuming the alternative functions and adhering to an alternative system of values that the system continues to operate.

Jessie Bernard suggests that although American society is characterized by achievement, specificity, universalism, individualism, and affective neutrality,[13] women's traditionally defined sphere is characterized by the reverse of each of these dominant patterns.[14] A woman is judged by what she is, rather than by her performance.[15] Her relationships are expected to be diffuse rather than specific or contractual; her morality is to be particularistic, emphasizing personal loyalty above abstract principles.[16] She is also expected to have a greater orientation to the collectivity (marriage, family, other groups) than to her own self-interest.[17] She is expected to demonstrate affectivity, or emotionalism, in a wide range of relationships rather than to emphasize neutral or impersonal relationships. As such, women and men can be seen as inhabiting two different worlds, one particularistic and the other universalistic. However, Bernard argues, the universalistic world has the advantage as American society becomes ever more contractual and impersonal. Despite the societal lack of emphasis on relationships built on love and/or duty, women are still expected to act out of these motives.[18]

The "ideal woman"—the traditionally esteemed ideal wife-mother figure—does not and cannot live according to dominant cultural values, but is required to operate under quite a different standard. Further, a woman is at once applauded for living by this secondary standard and denigrated for failure to do better. She is criticized for not being independent and assertive and logical, although she is programmed not to be. Therefore, she either does not attempt to live up to dominant standards and accepts (and rationalizes her acceptance of) a different set of standards, or she may try to live up to dominant standards and fail.

Eliot Liebow's "shadow system" of values suggests another possibility. Do most women actually use the dominant cultural ideal as their referent, or do they have their own separate, distinct system of values? Is the behavior of women a way of realizing distinctive values and goals of their own "subculture," or is it a way of concealing their failure to achieve the goals and values of the larger society? There seems to be a certain amount of evidence to support either position. It is possible to view the same behavior as explainable in different ways. For instance, women placing a positive value on self-sacrifice, non-aggressiveness, and supportiveness may be evidence of a true alternative value system for women. On the other hand, valuing these characteristics may be only a rationalization of defeat and an anticipation of failure resulting from subscribing to other values. At this particular time in history, it may appear that newly liberated American women are striving for middle-class, dominant values including success, achievement, competition, power, and so on. However, much questioning of these values is appearing in the writing of American feminists, perhaps reflecting the existence of an ongoing alternative system of values.

Women who live under a double standard of values live in an alternative but not really opposed system of values. This double standard for American society was noted by de Tocqueville in the nineteenth century when he pointed out that self-determination and freedom from tyranny are values for men, while submission and dependence are required of women.[19] Parsons's analysis implicates a double standard wherein women are confined to a "separate but equal" value sphere, where different value patterns are appropriate for and expected of the two sex roles. Thus, women are not expected to learn the success values of the occupational sphere, and are not failures if they do not succeed according to this standard. However, all children, regardless of sex, are exposed to the same specific-universal-achievement value system. Therefore, although little girls early internalize the same dominant values as little boys, later they learn to incorporate opposed value patterns. Failing to live up to dominant standards is then seen only as a failure for *men*. Parsons might argue that women would continue to value all of the achievement oriented patterns *for their husbands*, but learn an entirely separate set of standards for themselves. Thus they would not lose their belief in the dominant value system, but simply would not apply them to their own lives.

The common opposition between male and female principles, between the standard and the Other, between doing and being, between Yang and Yin, have been applied in empirical research and have led to such distinctions as that of Erik Erikson's "outer space" orientation of men and "inner space" orientation of women,[20] or to David Guttman's autocentric and allocentric ego styles.[21] These distinctions are based on the opposition of competence, rationality, and assertion vs. warmth and expressiveness.

LEGITIMATION OF INSTITUTIONAL ARRANGEMENTS

The dual system of values described as the traditional value system has operated to legitimate sexist institutional arrangements in the family, education, the occupational world, and the political sphere. People have tended to accept a double standard of values wherein women were expected to be acquiescent, passive, supportive, dependent, and cooperative in response to men's active, aggressive, independent, competitive behavior. As a result, women have been defined as being unsuited for the rigors of the competitive occupational and political worlds, have been channeled into certain areas of education, and have been expected to be naturally suited to the nurturing home-maker role. This dual system of values has been internalized by most persons in American society, simply because we are socialized to believe in these values and accept them. The values eventually can become part of a person's personality, providing the motivations for future actions. However, this double standard seems inadequate for present needs, for both women and men.

Women, as they move into the labor force and higher education and become exposed to feminist arguments, seem to begin to apply the dominant value system more to themselves. However, there are a variety of qualities which are necessary and desirable in human life, and not all of them are subsumed under what we have here considered the dominant value orientation of American society. Many of the "masculine" traits and values may not be particularly healthy for either sex, while some of the "feminine" traits (such as supportiveness and gentleness) have come to be seen as important for all.

CONCLUSION

The basic personality of the adult is developed through a process of internalizing the achievement values of American society. In this process, the capacity for independent achievement is learned by the child through the application by the parents of "conditional love." The parents withhold or grant love to the child on the basis of how closely that child approximates what they believe to be ideal behavior. Thus children learn the value orientations of the adult world and learn acceptance of adult masculine and feminine roles.[22]

Women may share the core values of equality and achievement, but these values may be reinterpreted for them.[23] There may be two separate value systems, one dominant and the other alternative, but girls are taught the dominant standard along with boys, thus receiving conflicting messages over which standard to adopt. While girls are usually rewarded for conforming to a "feminine" standard and punished for being too "masculine," they are also criticized for *not* being sufficiently masculine in the areas of dependence, logic, and emotionality. As Karen Sacks has said, "womanly temperaments" fight a losing battle, and a womanly emphasis on human interpersonal relations (as opposed to manly commodity relations), rank low in American society. Material survival aspects are at odds with the "womanly qualities" of warmth, supportiveness, and other-directedness.[24]

Dominant American values have been described here as including achievement and success, independence, progress, rationality, and equality. Traditional women's values, if there are a set of values representing an alternative system, would emphasize none of these things, except insofar as they would be considered valuable for men. However, it should be obvious that conditions and values are changing, and it seems unlikely that most American women would fail to believe that dominant values could apply to them as well as to men. Institutions are changing, perhaps too rapidly for values to match them. Structural changes require role changes and may in time require value changes.[25] Without changes in institutions, values are unlikely to change, as the two support each other.

If the society is to keep up with the possible future changes in women's participation in the social institutions, the need for change in the value system is apparent. However, the change could come in changing men, changing women, or changing both. Another possibility is that of changing basic values themselves. This would include questioning such core values as competition, the profit motive, progress and achievement, and suggesting as replacements humanity, feeling, caring and cooperating. The value of "success" itself would be examined as persons of both sexes suffer from not being able to live up to the dominant standards and thus not being "successful." The result of an altered set of values which followed for greater individual variation would eliminate the necessity for dominant and variant value systems. Because of its flexibility, the value system could be applied to persons of varying temperaments and abilities, without devaluing necessary, but presently secondary, qualities.

NOTES

1. See, for instance, Dale Neubauer, *Ideology and Society* (Morristown, N.J.: General Learning Press, 1975), p. 4.
2. Alexis de Tocqueville, *Democracy in America,* Vol. II (New York: Vintage, 1945), p. 104.
3. Ibid., p. 212.
4. Ibid., p. 213.
5. Geoffrey Gorer, *The American People: A Study in National Character,* rev. ed. (New York: W. W. Norton, 1964), pp. 151, 154.
6. Ibid., p. 219.
7. Robin Williams, *American Society* (New York: Knopf, 1952).
8. Florence Rockwood Kluckhohn, "Dominant and Substitute Profiles of Cultural Orientations: Their Significance for the Analysis of Social Structure," *Social Forces* 28 (May 1950), pp. 376–393.
9. Clyde Kluckhohn, Henry A. Murray, and David M. Schneider, ed., *Personality in Nature, Society and Culture,* 2d ed. (New York: Knopf, 1953).
10. Florence Rockwood Kluckhohn, "American Women and American Values," in *Facing the Future's Risks,* ed. Lyman Bryson (New York: Harper and Bros., 1953).
11. Kluckhohn, "Dominant and Variant Value Orientations," in Kluckhohn et al., op. cit.
12. Kluckhohn, in Bryson, op. cit.
13. Adapted from the typology of Talcott Parsons, *The Social System* (New York: Free Press, 1951).
14. Jessie Bernard, *Women and the Public Interest* (Chicago: Aldine-Atherton, 1971).
15. For a further discussion of the "being" vs. "doing" distinction, see Nancy Chodorow, "Being and Doing: A Cross-Cultural Examination of the Socialization of Males and Females," in *Woman in Sexist Society,* ed. Vivian Gornick and Barbara K. Moran (New York: New American Library, Signet Books, 1971).
16. See especially Freud on women's lesser sense of justice, in his *New Introductory Lectures* of 1932; or Schopenhauer's views discussed by Wolfgang Lederer, in *The Fear of Women* (New York: Harcourt Brace Jovanovich, 1968), p. 92.
17. For a full discussion of the woman's self-sacrifice and subjugation as fulfilling, see Helene Deutsch, *The Psychology of Women,* Vols. I and II (New York: Bantam, 1973).
18. Bernard, op. cit., p. 115.
19. De Tocqueville, op. cit.
20. Erik Erikson, *Childhood and Society* (New York: W. W. Norton and Co., 1950).

21. David Guttman, "Female Ego Styles and Generational Conflict," in *Feminine Personality and Conflict*, ed. Judith M. Bardwick, Elizabeth Douvan, Matina S. Horner, and David Guttman (Belmont, Calif.: Brooks/Cole Publ. Co., 1970).

22. Parsons, op. cit., pp. 218, 221, 224.

23. For a development of this argument, see Cynthia Fuchs Epstein, *Woman's Place: Options and Limits in Professional Careers* (Berkeley: University of California Press, 1971), pp. 40–41.

24. Karen Sacks, "Social Bases for Sexual Equality: A Comparative View," in *Sisterhood Is Powerful*, ed. Robin Morgan (New York: Vintage, 1970).

25. For other discussions of the culture and values of women, see Ann Battle-Sister, "Conjectures on the Female Culture," *Journal of Marriage and Family* 33 (1971), pp. 411–420. Battle-Sister finds that women have no independent culture in a positive sense, and that male values define women. Diana W. Warshay, "Sex Differences in Language Style," in *Toward A Sociology of Women*, ed. Constantina Safilios-Rothschild (Lexington, Mass.: Xerox College Publishing, 1972), pp. 3–9, finds evidence of different cultural expectations and value orientations for the two sexes.

ADDITIONAL REFERENCES

1. De Beauvoir, Simone. *The Second Sex*. New York, Bantam, 1970, for a full discussion of the woman as Other.

2. Hyman, Herbert H. "The Value Systems of Different Classes." *Class, Status and Power*, 2d ed. ed. Reinhard Bendix and S. M. Lipset. New York, Free Press, 1966.

3. Inkeles, Alex. "Some Sociological Observations on Culture and Personality Studies." *Personality in Nature, Society and Culture*, 2d ed., ed. Clyde Kluckhohn, Henry A. Murray, and David M. Schneider. New York, Knopf, 1953, 1971.

4. Janeway, Elizabeth. *Man's World, Woman's Place: A Study in Social Mythology*. New York: Dell, 1971, p. 100.

5. Kouidis, Virginia M. "American Character vs. the Ideal Woman." *Women and Public Policy: A Humanistic Perspective*. ed. Mildred H. Lavin and Clara H. Olsen. Iowa City: University of Iowa Institute of Public Affairs, 1974.

6. Liebow, Eliot. *Tally's Corner: A Study of Negro Streetcorner Men*. Boston: Little, Brown, 1967.

7. Marx, Leo. *The Machine in the Garden: Technology and the Pastoral Ideal in America*. Oxford University Press, 1964.

8. Parsons, Talcott. *The Social System*. New York: Free Press, 1951.

9. Williams, Robin. *American Society*. New York: Knopf, 1952, chapter 11.

7
PERPETUATION OF
THE FEMININE ROLE

As women, we felt equal, but we didn't always know how to act equal.
—Susan Dollens

At birth the most important distinction commonly noted about the child is its sex. On the basis of sex, certain expectations are established. Specified actions are carried out toward the infant and expected of her or him, and clear limits are placed on behavior. Differential treatment of children begins so early that often the parents do not notice it. Indeed, parents often claim that they are making no distinctions between the sexes, but in fact most already have begun to channel their children into sex roles. For example, parents have already selected a sex-linked name, sent out birth announcements announcing a "bouncing baby boy" or a "sweet girl," painted the nursery an appropriate color, or purchased clothing and toys which are "for girls" or "for boys."

Moreover, as several studies document, treatment of the child may also differ by sex as, for instance, in the physical handling of boy and girl infants, differential body contact, cooing, talking to and the like.[1] Where differences between the sexes are found, the tendency is toward greater stimulation and handling of boys.[2] And regardless

From "Preface," by Susan Dollens in *Woman, Assert Yourself!* An Instructive Handbook produced by The First Assertive Rap Group of Seattle-King County NOW, The National Organization for Women, New York: Perennial Library, 1976, p. 13. Reprinted by permission.

of belief in the equality of treatment of their children, most parents cannot help but think (perhaps realistically) that they must raise their son to be relatively independent, while this is less important for their daughter. Thus girls and boys begin to be socialized at first contact with their environment into culturally defined norms of "masculinity" and "femininity." This socialization is often subtle, but the results for children are nonetheless profound: each child learns the expected actions, attitudes, goals, rights, obligations, and prestige which are associated with its sex.

In the process of socialization, it is clear that reality is socially constructed. As we said in Chapter One, expectations which were once no more than a social definition became "reified into unalterable reality," so that alternatives are infrequently presented and often negatively sanctioned. A sociological perspective seeks to cut through the facade of conventional explanations, particularly when those using them either have a vested interest in distorting reality or simply cannot see events from any but their own perspective. The sociological perspective attempts to see particular events in a larger context, to remove the blinders, and to look for explanations and functions of existing ideologies.

DIFFERENTIAL SOCIALIZATION

If women never seem to attain the kinds of positions in society that men attain, it is sensible to assume that some of the reasons are built into the structure of society. These reasons can be determined by analyzing the conditions under which people live and are reared. Socialization theory suggests why there are such great differences in the eventual achievements of women and men, because parents and others in the infant's social environment tend to foster different attitudes, behaviors, skills, and orientations in girls and boys. These are generally in accordance with societally defined expectations, and are further reinforced by the school, the media, and the child's peers. Along with ideas of appropriate (and inappropriate) behaviors for the sexes are transmitted an evaluation of which traits are "better" and which have higher status and prestige.

Research with very young children has shown that they can be aware of cultural definitions of masculinity and femininity by the age of two or three, even when role models provided by their own parents deviate from culturally prescribed roles.[3] For example, even if a mother works and the father performs domestic duties, their children will usually identify the stereotypic roles they feel are played by mothers and fathers in our society. Such early identification has profound consequences for children, since sex role learning is probably the most frequently and intensively reinforced of all role learning, both in terms of rewards for "appropriate" behavior and punishment for that which is not. In the late 1950's Sears et al. presented evidence that sex-typing behaviors were sanctioned through childrearing practices soon after infancy. Girls by the age of two had been consistently rewarded for dependency while boys had been so rewarded to a lesser degree and had on the contrary tended to be rewarded for overt acts of controlling the environment. Although most mothers in Sears's study did not recognize that they were fostering sex-typed behaviors, they were doing so through such means as dress, games, toys, chores, permitting aggression, demanding obedience, table manners, and neatness. They often also treated their boy children and girl children differently with regard to the method or use of punishment and the use of warmth and permissiveness.[4] Children, then, were simply observing those around them, internalizing what they observed, and coming to see themselves in terms of the reactions and treatments they received at the hands of others. Gradually the role behavior and expectations came to be taken for granted, to be seen as a "natural" part of one's makeup so that it was not only desirable that girls should be quiet and neat, boys rough and noisy, but that this was part of their inborn nature.

The habits, attitudes and behaviors associated with sex role learning become so ingrained that they come to seem "natural." Definitions of what is feminine and what is masculine are established and maintained by a societal ideal. Therefore, to say that a man is not "masculine" or a woman is not "feminine" means only that he or she is not conforming to what society defines as ideal masculine or feminine behavior.

There are a number of factors involved in the differential socialization of children. We have suggested here that direct shaping of behaviors by parents and direct reinforcement for appropriate behaviors are among the important influences on sex role learning. Another important body of research deals with observational learning, imitation and identification.[5] This line of research suggests that role-modeling is important in sex-role learning, and that children tend to imitate the parent of the same sex, thus learning "appropriate" behavior for their sex. The evidence on whether this is a natural tendency or not is unclear, but at least it seems to be the case that children tend to imitate the same sex model after age five.[6] It also appears that the child's behavior is not a copy of the model's behavior, but is rather a simplified version of what the child takes to be appropriate behavior.

One line of research which seems to be proving fruitful is that which deals with the idea of the development of the concept of sex role. Lawrence Kohlberg has suggested that it is not direct shaping or reinforcement, imitation or modeling which leads to sex role behavior, but it is the construction of a concept of what is appropriate behavior for one of his/her sex which determines the child's own subsequent self-socialization.[7] Children are encouraged to choose sex-appropriate activities and exert a certain amount of pressure against inappropriate activities.[8] Parents also provide themselves as models of feminine and masculine roles, and tend to be imitated by their same-sex children. However, perhaps most importantly, children themselves seem to learn what their sex identity is, what behavior is appropriate for their sex, and then to act in accordance with this concept.[9]

Childrearing practices in American society certainly cannot be said to be consistent or monolithic. Much of childrearing is somewhat haphazard, rather than rationally planned, and can be based on advice from friends, relatives, the mass media, "expert" advice in childrearing books, and from experience. Childhood experiences lay the groundwork for later developments, but they do not make up all of an adult personality, nor are they the same for all people in the same society or culture. There are wide variations in socialization practices by social class and by race or ethnic group. For example, lower classes seem to be more concerned with sex-typing and differentiation of roles.[10] And there are indications that black girls are encouraged to be more independent, strong, and resourceful than is the norm for white girls.[11] Despite all the variations, there seems to be a fairly common agreement in American society on a basic division of labor, and of functions, between the sexes.

Generally, sexual division of labor specifies that certain broad categories of tasks must be performed by men and other broad categories by women. For historical, biological, psychological, economic, and sociological reasons a sexual division of labor has existed in most societies at most times. The division of labor was apparently based on women's stronger ties to the home because of childbearing and men's relatively greater freedom. Today the division of labor refers to the sex-typing of jobs (discussed in Chapter Four) but also is related to what Bernard has called the "sexual specialization of functions."[12] One of the specialized functions is the supportive function, which arises out of the notion that there is a sexual division of labor based on differences in functions which are both necessary and functional for society. The supportive or "stroking" function, defined as peculiarly that of women, may arise from women's inherently more supportive and emotional nature, or it could be more a result of the sort of sexual division of labor and functions which arise as a "natural" process in the family.[13]

Girls and boys are also said to learn in different manners, again based on the sexual specialization of functions in the family. David Lynn argues that girls can learn the feminine role through imitation, by observation of a female figure who is present and available as a model. Because they do not need to abstract principles of the feminine role, their method of learning is one of "lesson learning." Boys develop their analytic and "problem solving" skills because of the absence of a male figure as a model to imitate. Since the boy is unable to see or understand what his father does (and learn the "role" of male), he develops a stereotyped and conventional idea of the masculine role, learning to identify with this *role,* rather than with a person.[14]

Lynn hypothesized that girls had an easier time identifying with their mothers than boys did with their fathers. This was both because of the greater availability of the female role model, and because the girl is not required to change her initial infant identification with her original role model (her mother). The boy must change from an identification with his mother to an identification with his father, and thus has greater difficulty becoming socialized, and a less clear early identification.[15]

Interestingly, Parsons, Lynn, and Freud are in agreement that this begins with an early identification with the mother, which later is replaced by identification with the father for boys. But where Lynn and Parsons both felt that girls would have a much easier time with identification and socialization, Freud found the process more difficult for girls. The girl must change her original "love object" (defined in terms of sexual desires) from her mother to her father, whereas the boy retains the original love object.[16] Most sex role learning theories seem to be based on the notion of the availability of a female role model, and of the unavailability of a male role model.

A drawback of many sex role socialization theories is their middle-class and contemporary bias. Lynn, for instance, overlooks the very large proportion of married women with children in the home who are working, and thus not supplying the role model which is so easily imitatable. Perhaps more importantly, he overlooks the fact that many fathers' jobs are not necessarily difficult to identify with or to observe. A relatively large proportion of men are not engaged in abstract, mysterious work which is unintelligible to the mind of a child, but are involved in farming, labor, or other occupations which are observable and imitatable. Are we to assume that boys with fathers who perform observable work develop less skill at abstracting and problem-solving, and instead show a more "feminine" pattern of "lesson-learning"? These theories also tend to overlook patterns in other times and places, particularly agrarian societies, where fathers and mothers are equally available as role models. The evidence seems to indicate that specialization of functions occurs almost everywhere, including societies in which there is no difference in availability of role models.

DEVELOPMENT OF SELF

Through interaction with significant others, the child learns both directly (by being told) and indirectly (by observation) how to act in various situations. Eventually the child learns how to regulate his or her own behavior. An important part of this process of self-regulation is the development of the self. The self emerges out of contact and communication with others. It arises out of a process of placing oneself in the place of the other and imagining his/her reactions. George Herbert Mead described this as a developmental process where first the young child *plays* at the role of another, and later *learns* an organization of roles, taking the attitudes of a number of others at the same time. Thus, all the factors which influence our socialization influence our conception of self, and our self-concept becomes an interpretation of all the reactions to ourselves we have encountered in social interaction.[17]

Negative Self-Concept

The point has often been made in writings on women that they suffer from negative, damaged, undeveloped, limited, assaulted, inferior, or low self-concepts. The belief that this is true is based on the fact that women do, on the whole, tend to denigrate members of their own sex, and if they hold their entire sex in low esteem, it follows that they also should hold themselves in low esteem.

Women's self-concept, like the self-concept of any person, is dependent on the reflected appraisals of themselves as seen through the reactions of others. "Selves" are developed in accordance with the opinions of themselves (as individuals and as women in general) that they learn as a result of interactions with others; the self is developed in social interaction. Females interact with others in their social environment and learn through the interaction that certain things are expected of them and, perhaps more important, that certain things are *not* expected of them. Over a period of time, they will come to incorporate this as reality and to react in the future as if the expectations were "true" and not socially or culturally derived and communicated. Therefore, although they are learning to display feminine behavior, they are also learning the societal evaluation of this behavior, and thus may learn to value "femininity" very highly. Most writings on this subject conclude that women are more negative or ambivalent about themselves and develop less self-esteem than do men. Self-concept, here, is defined as one's evaluation of oneself in terms of self-esteem, capability, desirable personal qualities and attributes, and a distinct identity. According to this definition, then, a person would have a low or negative self-concept if she thought herself to be incompetent, to be unable to cope with the normal world, or to have few desirable attributes.

If there is a "female self-concept," it is described as including the idea of the female self as more gentle, supportive, emotional, dependent, and less rational. It is not clear that the belief that one has these qualities is indicative of a "negative self-concept," or is related to low self-esteem. While research evidence points to the higher social desirability of so-called "masculine" qualities in others,[18] it is not completely clear that women devalue these feminine qualities in themselves.

One of the pieces of research which actually attempted to measure *self*-evaluations was done by Edward M. Bennett and Larry R. Cohen.[19] Their results contradicted many commonplace assumptions about self-concept. They concluded that female self-concept was *more* clearly established than that of men, and they found women scoring themselves higher on such things as autonomy and uniqueness, while men scored themselves higher on, for instance, egocentrism and personal conservatism.

Ordinary means of attempting to measure self-concept, including use of the semantic differential technique, check-off lists of adjectives, or statements about the self, generally reveal little or no difference.[20] John P. McKee and Alex C. Sheriffs found that women in their study used more unfavorable adjectives to describe themselves than did men, but this difference was not large.[21] Other ways of measuring self-concept, such as the Twenty Statements Test (TST), have found differences in the way the sexes respond, but the meaning of the differences is not always clear. For instance, Harold A. Mulford and Winfield W. Salisbury found that adult women were less likely to describe themselves by gender than were men.[22] Carl Couch, studying families with high role specialization, presented the plausible explanation that these women's low self-esteem about being female could have explained why many women did not use their sex as an identifier.[23] However, this apparently logical conclusion is less credible when one considers the fact that the opposite has also been found, and college-age women mention their sex *more* often than do men. Manford Kuhn,[24] for instance, found that female undergraduates mentioned their sex significantly more often than did male undergraduates, and my own research has found the same. Kuhn suggested that sex mention by women may be related to their minority group status or to the salience of their sex during the period of dating and courtship. My own conclusion was that sex mention seemed to be somewhat related to the consciousness and salience of one's sex, either because one was very traditionally feminine or because one was very "liberated" or very much into women's movement activities or beliefs. It is not clear from TST evidence what any of the differences mean, other than that people tend to mention roles and characteristics which are *salient* to them, for whatever reason.

Several reasonable arguments have been made about the effects of being female on self-esteem. First, it has been concluded that a woman's self is defined by her relationship to a man, because of her tendency to neglect her own future plans and sacrifice her own development to allow for her husband and family. As a result, a woman may develop a less sure sense of self, of who she is, and of how she sees herself. Her self-concept then might be expected to be less stable and more ambiguous.[25]

Second, it is generally held that the struggle for autonomy against parental pressure results in an earlier development of self-esteem. In this event, boys would be more likely to develop a sense of self-esteem earlier, as they are allowed to demonstrate autonomy against parental pressure earlier, and the outcome in terms of long-range self-esteem might be enhanced because of their greater success in resisting parental pressure and being allowed further autonomy. The dependent person, with decisions made for her and severe limits placed on her, might then be expected to be not only less autonomous but less sure of herself, with a resultant weakness of self-concept.[26]

Third, cultural values tend to emphasize achievement, competition, and aggression, but these values do not apply equally to males and females. Women, then, might be expected to develop lower or more negative self-concepts if they fail to live up to those general societal standards. On the other hand, they may also suffer from fear of rejection if they do strive for these standards, since they are not considered feminine. The result, then, could be a damaged self-concept based on the expected disapproval of conduct.[27]

During the process of sex role socialization, females are exposed to attitudes and expectations about women which may lead them to think of themselves as secondary or marginal members of society. In 1951, Helen Mayer Hacker described her sociological theory of the marginality of woman's status in a masculine society. Although women are not numerically a minority, Hacker felt that the presence of discrimination created a sociological minority group:

A minority group is any group of people who because of their physical or cultural characteristics, are singled out from the others in the society in which they live for differential and unequal treatment, and who therefore regard themselves as objects of collective discrimination.[28]

Hacker noted that while in 1951 few women seemed to think of themselves as members of a minority group, women displayed many of the psychological characteristics which have been imputed to self-conscious minority groups. One of the most important of these characteristics was group self-hatred. By self-hatred Hacker meant that women denigrate other women and tend to accept the stereotypes of women. Women often disassociate themselves from the group, or if they identify with the group, blame themselves for things which are often the result of institutional sexism and oppression.

Group self-hatred is related to the development of self-concept through the socialization process. The marginal woman who suffers conflict, anxiety, resentment and self-hate rises out of stereotyped rejections and acceptances. She is rejected in non-traditional roles, and accepted only in limited roles with stereotyped behavior. The self-hatred she feels is based on her acceptance of qualities which are generally labeled as inferior. These qualities include lower intelligence, illogic, emotional instability, weakness, and inconsistency. Women also learn "accommodation attitudes." This means using "feminine wiles," flattering, appearing helpless. These manipulative practices are used to outwit men and get what they want. However, they may also lead women to think of all women as actually deceitful and manipulative and therefore contemptible, leading to a hatred of their own group.

It is not at all clear that any of the above occurs, or that if it does, it results in a lower, more negative, more tentative, less stable, less secure, damaged, or weak self-concept for women. It appears more likely that many women learn to disparage their own group (or learn group self-hatred), while retaining positive evaluations of themselves. If group self-hatred carried over to their evaluations of themselves, we should find that women who have less positive attitudes toward women as a group also have lower self-concepts. Findings from my own research in this area indicate that this is not true. I did not find women's self-evaluations to be any lower than men's, and there were no significant differences on self-evaluation scores for women with highly "liberal" attitudes toward women's roles as compared to women having neutral or traditional attitudes.[29] Similar results have been found by Janet T. Spence, Robert Helmreich and Joy Stapp, who have demonstrated no relationship between their self-esteem measure and their Attitudes Toward Women scale.[30]

Derogation of Women
The acceptance of the stereotypes and inferior status of women is so widespread that it has led to the tendency of women to agree with the statement that "women have only themselves to blame for their own problems." It has also led to what has been termed the Queen Bee Syndrome.[31] According to the description of this syndrome, the woman who has made her way up in a man's world tacitly joins with the traditional women to oppose feminism. Her attitude is that if she can do it without a movement to help her, so can other women. Other women who don't make it, or who complain about discrimination and sexism, are dismissed as whiners and neurotics. The Queen Bee has succeeded as an individual, and rejects the women's movement assumption that women's problems are external in origin, rather than of their own making. The Queen Bee instead reasons that a woman's shortcomings and inferior positions are indeed her own fault, and if other women were superior persons like she is, they could make it too. Therefore, the fact that there are so few women in high positions simply demonstrates that there are very few superior or even highly competent women.

The argument is understandable from the Queen Bee's point of view. She can congratulate herself that she deserves to be where she is because of her own personal talent and strivings. It is ego-gratifying to believe that you have succeeded because of your own talents and brilliance. It is much harder to recognize the part played by situational and chance factors of socialization, the environment and discrimination, or the fact that now and then a token person is allowed to make it. It is interesting that people who do well attribute their success to personal qualities, while failures are blamed on aspects of the situation.

Although the successful woman is in a good position to advance the cause of women, she is very often unlikely to do this. The refusal is partly a desire to protect her own exclusive and privileged position, and partly out of her general contempt for women. She identifies with males, and through this "identification with the oppressor" rejects her own group and contributes to their lack of solidarity. But the Queen Bee Syndrome has a middle range counterpart which may pose a greater threat to the long range goals of persons interested in human liberation. These are the women who do not reject other women but who do not feel that oppression is real. This type of woman feels that she has done well enough and is happy being what she is, and that a woman of talent and ability can accomplish anything she wants, can overcome any barriers to achievement. Besides, she would argue, the barriers are not a real problem now, as women are given equal opportunities everywhere. There are certainly more important issues than feminism.

While this argument may sound sensible to some, it fails when analyzed. As we have already seen, oppression is very real. Barriers not only continue to exist, but there are some indications that the status of women has not improved significantly, if at all, since the beginning of Women's Liberation activities.[32] The fact is that perhaps a woman of *talent* and *ability* (and possibly motivation and intestinal fortitude as well) *can* accomplish what she wants, but it requires fortuitous socialization experiences, chance and situational factors to put most women into the position of recognizing their own talents, abilities, and options. Also, it is the talented and able woman who achieves—not the average woman. This means that most women, by definition, will not achieve much. On the other hand, mediocre men commonly achieve certain goals without encountering institutionalized barriers and oppressive socialization practices.

Women do not seem to see themselves in the light in which they see other women. Each woman sees herself as worthwhile and individualistic, but at least to some extent sees other women as a stereotyped group. And those who have the most positive, least stereotyped views of women as a group do not appear to have "better" or "higher" self-concepts as a result. The Queen Bee Syndrome therefore may not only be a problem of the highly successful woman, but of women in general.

Why do women discriminate against each other? Why do women often seem to have contempt for other women? Why is "sisterhood" such a difficult ideal to attain? The answer seems to lie in the isolation of women and lack of perception of any source of cohesion or solidarity. Women have not been encouraged to share or to come together in their own behalf, and in fact have been encouraged to be competitive with each other, since the goal was to beat the other woman out for the ultimate prize, usually a man. Also, an ingrained belief in her own inferiority and superficiality and a belief in man's superiority can lead a woman to disregard the efforts and accomplishments of other women. Philip Goldberg's study of women's prejudiced judgments of the work of other women suggested that women did believe work supposedly done by men to be superior,[33] although this finding has been challenged in the last few years.[34] But women are still often encouraged to think of themselves as unique if they are competent or talented, which tends to create divisiveness and competition. A woman must be *more* than a woman to be worthwhile, and must never be "just like a woman." But by making herself an exception and putting herself above other women, she is participating in her own oppression.[35]

Stigmatized Identity

Although the "stigma" of being female is not comparable to that of having a serious disability or of belonging to a despised minority group, there is some truth in the idea of female status as stigmatized identity. Erving Goffman defines a stigma as an attribute that is deeply discrediting. He argues that a stigmatized person is, by definition, not quite human, is therefore held to be inferior, and is discriminated against.[36] While this description may be overstated in the case of sex, certain similarities are apparent, and the results of stigmatization and the reactions to it seem very similar. Goffman argues that because of the discrimination and prejudice against all stigmatized persons, the particular person may learn to feel shame over his/her own attributes and may respond in a number of ways, several of which are particularly pertinent in the case of women. Two of these are: overcompensating, especially in excelling in other areas; and using it as an excuse to escape from competition and to be protected from responsibility. The first response may take the form of becoming a super "womanly" woman, excelling in all spheres which can be defined as "feminine," and eschewing competition in what are often considered masculine areas. The second, withdrawal from the arena of competition, is more common. The other responses Goffman mentions are not entirely inapplicable either, as they include the attempt to correct the deficiency, or to return to "normal," which, while impossible in the case of women, can be seen in attempts to be as much like men as possible. Another response is viewing the stigma as a blessing in disguise, or learning from suffering, which may be seen in the case of the martyred, self-sacrificing woman who only expects to be rewarded in heaven. Another response is in re-assessing "normals" and their limitations, which can be seen in the case of women who question the natural superiority of men and see their abilities and weaknesses within a more equal perspective. Finally, Goffman mentions the possibility of withdrawal or defensive cowering, as in anticipation of poor treatment. This may be related to the hesitation of many women to enter into situations of interaction with men, or to hold back comments in discussions with men.

Goffman's argument is that the stigmatized person learns and incorporates, through a process of socialization, the standards of the normal. Applied to women, this means she learns she possesses the stigma and learns the consequences of possessing it. She will then apply all the prejudices she has learned about similarly stigmatized people to herself, resulting in a relatively low opinion of herself. Goffman concludes that most stigmatized persons feel ambivalence about their own selves because of society's standards and their inability to conform to those standards. Society's idea of "good adjustment" (or in our example, being adjusted to one's femininity) is the individual's acceptance of herself as the same as "normals", while at the same time voluntarily withholding herself from those situations in which it would be difficult for "normals" (men) to show their similar acceptance. In other words, she shouldn't burden men with her presence when it is not wanted, thus never confronting men with their own limited tolerance.

CONCLUSION
The processes of socialization and the development of self can contribute to the perpetuation of the "feminine" role, limiting and oppressing women. During the socialization process, children learn the proper role to play in American society and develop a concept of appropriate activities and beliefs which not only narrow their possibilities but which may be negative and damaging. Although it is not clear that these negative images affect women's personal self-esteem, they have had the effect of creating prejudice against women as a group. As we have seen in the preceding chapters, it appears that socialization practices and the beliefs they instill in girls affect the degree to which women feel competent to participate equally in societally important activities and various social arenas. There are obvious institutional barriers limiting the equality of women in American society, and discrimination against women continues in the job market, in education, and in the political world partly because of low evaluations of women as a social category and partly because of the expectations girls learn about the feminine role.

Sex-role socialization theory can present an oversocialized view of women, exaggerating the consistency of the pressures on women to adopt the feminine role, the overall effectiveness of the process, and its complete internalization.[37] In reality, there is a good deal of overlap in socialization practices for girls and boys; girls are often rewarded and reinforced for behaviors and attitudes which might be considered masculine. Nevertheless, the structural or institutional barriers and the processes of socialization are inseparable. Without sex-stereotyped childrearing practices, the "feminine role" would not be perpetuated.

NOTES

1. Howard A. Moss, "Sex, Age and State as Determinants of Mother-Infant Interaction," *Merrill-Palmer Quarterly* 13 (1967), pp. 19–36; Susan Goldberg and Michael Lewis, "Play Behavior in the Year-Old Infant: Early Sex Differences," *Child Development* 40 (1969), pp. 21–30; Michael Lewis, "Culture and Gender Roles," *Psychology Today* 5 (May 1972), pp. 54–57; Michael Lewis, "State as an Infant-Environment Interaction: An Analysis of Mother-Infant Behavior as a Function of Sex," *Merrill-Palmer Quarterly* 18 (1972), pp. 95–121; Jerome Kagan, "The Emergence of Sex Differences," *School Review* (February 1972), pp. 217–227.

2. Eleanor Emmons Maccoby and Carol Nagy Jacklin, *The Psychology of Sex Differences* (Stanford, Calif.: Stanford University Press, 1974).

3. Jerome Kagan, "Acquisition and Significance of Sex Typing and Sex Role Identity," in *Review of Child Development Research*, ed. M. L. Hoffman and L. W. Hoffman (New York: Russell Sage, 1964), pp. 137–167; Robert R. Sears, Eleanor Maccoby, and H. Levin, *Patterns of Child Rearing* (Evanston, Ill.: Row, Peterson, 1957).

4. Sears et al., op. cit.

5. Kagan, op. cit.; Sears et al., 1964, op. cit.; Lawrence Kohlberg, "The Cognitive-Developmental Analysis of Children's Sex-Role Concepts and Attitudes," in *The Development of Sex Differences*, ed. Eleanor Maccoby (Stanford, Calif.: Stanford University Press, 1966); Walter Mischel, "Sex-Typing and Socialization," in *Carmichael's Manual of Child Psychology*, ed. P. H. Mussen (New York: Wiley, 1970); P. H. Mussen, "Early Sex-Role Development," in *Handbook of Socialization Theory and Research*, ed. D. A. Goslin (Chicago: Rand McNally, 1969); A. Bandura and R. Walters, *Social Learning and Personality Development* (New York: Holt, Rinehart and Winston, 1963).

6. Maccoby and Jacklin, op. cit.

7. Kohlberg, op. cit.

8. Maccoby and Jacklin, op. cit., p. 339.

9. Ibid.; see especially pp. 364–365.

10. Melvin L. Kohn, "Social Class and Parental Values," *American Journal of Sociology* 64 (January 1959), pp. 337–351; Mayer L. Rabban, "Sex Role Identification in Young Children in Two Diverse Social Groups," *Genetics Psychology Monographs* 42 (1950), pp. 81–158.

11. Joyce Ladner, *Tomorrow's Tomorrow: The Black Woman* (Garden City, N.Y.: Doubleday, 1971).

12. Jessie Bernard, *Women and the Public Interest* (Chicago: Aldine-Atherton, 1971).

13. Talcott Parsons, "The American Family: Its Relations to Personality and to the Social Structure," in *Family, Socialization and Interaction Process*, ed. Talcott Parsons and Robert F. Bales (New York: Free Press, 1955).

14. David Lynn, "The Process of Learning Parental and Sex-Role Identification," *Journal of Marriage and Family* 28 (1966), pp. 446–470.

15. Parsons, op. cit.

16. Sigmund Freud, "Some Psychological Consequences of the Anatomical Distinction between the Sexes," (1925) and "Female Sexuality," (1931) in Sigmund Freud, *Sexuality and the Psychology of Love* (New York: Collier Books, 1963). Freud felt that there were other reasons for women's greater difficulties with identification, notably the need to change the erogenous zone from the clitoris to the vagina.

17. George Herbert Mead, *Mind, Self and Society* (Chicago: University of Chicago Press, 1934).

18. John P. McKee and Alex C. Sheriffs, "Men's and Women's Beliefs, Ideals, and Self-Concepts," *American Journal of Sociology* 64 (1959), pp. 356–364; Paul Rosenkrantz, Susan Vcgel, Helen Bee, Inge Broverman, and Donald M. Broverman, "Sex Role Stereotypes and Self-Concepts in College Students," *Journal of Consulting and Clinical Psychology* 32 (1968), pp. 287–293.

19. Edward M. Bennett and Larry R. Cohen, "Men and Women: Personality Patterns and Contrasts," *Genetics Psychology Monographs* 59 (1959), pp. 101–155.

20. Maccoby and Jacklin, op. cit., come to the same conclusion.

21. McKee and Sherriffs, op. cit.

22. Harold A. Mulford and Winfield W. Salisbury III, "Self Conceptions in a General Population," *Sociological Quarterly* 5 (Winter 1964), pp. 35–46.

23. Carl Couch, "Family Role Specialization and Self Attitudes in Children," *Sociological Quarterly* 3 (1962), pp. 115–121.

24. Manford Kuhn, "Self Attitudes by Age, Sex, and Professional Training," *Sociological Quarterly* 1 (January 1960), pp. 39–55.

25. Judith Bardwick and Elizabeth Douvan, "Ambivalence: The Socialization of Women," in *Woman in Sexist Society*, ed. Vivian Gornick and Barbara Moran (New York: Basic Books, 1971), pp. 225–241.

26. Clarice Stasz Stoll, *Female and Male: Socialization, Social Roles, and Social Structure* (Dubuque, Iowa: Wm. C. Brown Co., 1974).

27. Ibid.

28. Helen Mayer Hacker, "Women as a Minority Group," *Social Forces* 30 (October 1951), pp. 60–69.

29. Carol A. Whitehurst, "An Empirical Investigation of Women's Self-Evaluation," unpublished (July 1976).

30. Janet T. Spence, Robert Helmreich, and Joy Stapp, "Ratings of Self and Peers on Sex Role Attributes and Their Relation to Self-Esteem and Conceptions of Masculinity and Femininity," *Journal of Personal and Social Psychology* 32 (1975), pp. 29–39.

31. Graham Staines, Carol Tavris, and Toby Epstein Jayaratne, "The Queen Bee Syndrome," in *The Female Experience, Psychology Today* (1973).

32. See Clare Boothe Luce, "The 21st-Century Woman—Free At Last?" *Saturday Review World*, 24 August 1974, pp. 58–62.

33. Philip Goldberg, "Are Women Prejudiced Against Women?" *Trans-Action* 5 (April 1968), pp. 28–30.

34. Gail I. Pheterson, Sara B. Kiesler, and Philip O. Goldberg, "Evaluation of the Performance of Women as a Function of Their Sex, Achievement, and Personal History," *Journal of Personal and Social Psychology* 19 (July 1971), pp. 114–118; Debbie Halon Soto and Claudia Cole, "Prejudice Against Women: A New Perspective," *Sex Roles* 1 (December 1975), pp. 385–393.

35. Shulamith Firestone, *The Dialectic of Sex* (New York: Wm. Morrow, 1970), pp. 278–282.

36. Erving Goffman, *Stigma: Notes on the Management of Spoiled Identity* (Englewood Cliffs, N.J.: Prentice-Hall, 1963).

37. Lenore Weitzman, "Sex-Role Socialization," in *Women: A Feminist Perspective*, ed. Jo Freeman (Palo Alto, Calif.: Mayfield, 1975), pp. 105–144.

ADDITIONAL REFERENCES

1. Chafetz, Janet Saltzman. *Masculine/Feminine or Human?* Itasca, Ill.: F. E. Peacock, 1974, p. 89.

2. Epstein, Cynthia Fuchs. *Woman's Place.* Berkeley, Calif.: University of California Press, 1971, p. 25.

3. Whitehurst, Carol A. "An Empirical Investigation of Women's Self-Evaluation." unpublished, July 1976.

8
PSYCHOLOGICAL OPPRESSION

> *The universal sway of the feminine stereo-*
> *type is the single most important factor in*
> *male and female woman-hatred.*
> —*Germaine Greer*

Throughout this book, we have discussed the sources of institutional oppression of women and the ways in which these oppressive forces have been perpetuated. Socialization and sex-role learning have nurtured these forces, and they have been reinforced in the media and supported by cultural values. As a result, a condition can develop which is often referred to as "psychological oppression," a woman's conviction that there are many things which she cannot and/or should not attempt to do, simply because she is incapable, by virtue of being a woman. Psychological oppression is created in women when they learn to see themselves as limited beings, incapable of many activities, particularly societally important activities involving power, decision-making, and leadership. Psychological oppression is learning contempt for one's kind and devaluing females and feminine qualities. If carried to extremes, this can mean self-hatred which may lead to timidity, lack of confidence, fear, hesitancy, and insecurity.

A further type of psychological oppression is the feeling of being caged, being kept on a leash, being limited and stunted. This is manifested in boredom, frustration, anomie, and the "problem that has no name." Psychological oppression also means lack of identity, of knowing who you are and what you want to be and do. It manifests itself in anxiety and fear of being abandoned, of growing old, of not being loved, of being mistreated or assaulted. This oppression has been referred to as the "psychic cost of being a woman," which means never being able to fully accept herself as a totally successful human being.

Thus, psychological oppression exists when a woman has internalized her oppression. Not only are her behaviors defined, limited, and changed by the external forces of dominant institutions, but her feelings, attitudes and psychic life are similarly limited by internalized beliefs. Creating a sense of inferiority and incompetence within a person is far more effective than any external controls, in the form of rules, laws, and restrictive norms, could ever be. These external controls may have the effect of discriminating against women and keeping them in their place, but they must be accompanied by internal controls which convince them that this is the only place they are capable of occupying. Thus it is believing and accepting that women are limited, inferior creatures which is psychologically oppressive, not institutional and external oppression per se.

> *"The most corrosive effect of the discrimination against women is the psychological effect it has of reducing a sense of personal competence, of encouraging women to disqualify themselves before the male managerial world has a chance to rebuff them."* [1]

Not all women are socialized and programmed in the same ways, but the extreme end of the "brainwashing" continuum would create psychological cowardice, a fear to take available options or an inability even to see the options or to believe any options can represent a viable alternative. However, this extreme of psychological oppression is seldom reached, although most women suffer from certain aspects, at certain times. Even so, for those who do see and seek other options, the route may seem impassable unless they are willing to reject "feminine" values and women as a group, while taking on male-defined success values. Thus, any woman, whether "brainwashed" or not, can become psychologically scarred: by feelings of inferiority if she does not compete, or by becoming hard from fighting for the right to compete and be accepted.

> *The most insidious aspect of this caste system is the psychological effect it has on most females. For many it serves a self-fulfilling prophecy, rendering them virtually unfit to assume anything other than the passive, dependent role for which they have been programmed. For countless others it entails perpetual anxiety and guilt over what they are*

and do versus what they "ought to be" according to society. But for some, and especially those who "make it" in the males' world, it entails assuming the values of the upper caste and denigrating all aspects of femaleness. [2]

ROOTS OF PSYCHOLOGICAL OPPRESSION

Throughout history, woman has been presented often in mythology as the outsider, the unknown and unknowable. Much of the source of this mystery seems to lie in women's sexual and reproductive functions which long have been surrounded by rituals and taboos. According to Wolfgang Lederer's research in *The Fear of Women*, men experience awe and dread of women, both of which are rooted in the biological differences between the sexes which seem to render women eternally incomprehensible, mysterious and strange. The awe manifests itself in the worship of fertility goddesses, but woman's powers to create, nourish, and sustain are also the source of man's fear. He fears the overwhelming importance of maternity and his own relative unimportance, as well as the potentially smothering, oppressive experience of the maternal instinct. A woman may be considered as the Eternal Female, serene, content, never-changing, and also as conservative and practical, tying him down and rejecting his idealism.

Lederer speculates further that women's sexual capabilities have also been the source of fear and awe. On one hand she is the source of all pleasure, but on the other she has been feared as having insatiable sexual appetites. Because man can never match her capacities, admiration may take the form of fear of his own sexual inadequacy. A number of myths, such as those of Eve and Pandora, suggest that sin and death were brought into the world by women. Associating sin with female sexuality led to the view of woman as temptress, the obstacle to man's purity and then his downfall. A part of woman's early Christian image was based on this association of her with evil, and as a secondary, lowly creature, without many of man's higher qualities. In the Aristotelian conception of the universe, women were assigned the characteristics of the lower self—the body without the soul—while men were the rationalized self. The Christian ethic established the connection between women, sex and sin, and partly from this source came the dual image of woman as evil seductress or pure virgin. This dichotomy is clearly shown in the Virgin Mary, a symbol of virtue, and the witch, a symbol of evil. Thus, within religions, goodness in women came to be synonymous with virginity, evil with sexual experience.

Images of women have been ambivalent, and for every role there has been a positive and negative view; for instance, as givers of life and nurturers, or as deniers of satisfaction and givers of pain. Thus women, more than men, are not presented merely as people—part good and part evil—but as stereotyped, one-dimensional characters, on the basis of their sexuality or lack of it. Images of women are still often either/or: if she is not a virgin, she is a whore; if not an earth mother, a witch or a bitch. Those images are used as propaganda to keep women in their place and blind them to the nature of their oppression.[3]

Western literature has perpetuated the dual image of woman as Light Lady versus Dark Lady. If women were not pure, virtuous, and basically asexual, they were untamed, earthy, and seductive. Light Ladies were heroines representing Civilization, the cultured and genteel forces of society, the "feminizing" influences. They were almost always blonde, fair-skinned, delicate, and virginal. Dark Ladies represented Nature, a wild, threatening, but appealing wilderness. They were usually brunette, voluptuous, unconventional, and often sexually experienced. The conflict between the undisciplined dark forces and the controlled, contained civilized influences usually was resolved in favor of the delicate, pale, submissive woman.[4]

While the dual image of women has been used to stereotype and confine them, even more important is the fact that the male stereotype, characteristics and role have been considered more important than those of the female. Simone de Beauvoir points out that in human society the male principle, Transcendence, won out over the female principle, Immanence, originally because of men's superior strength, fewer physical limitations, and greater independence. As a result, man is defined as the Subject, the Absolute—both the positive and the neutral. Woman is the Other, the negative, the incidental and inessential. Woman is different, mysterious, unknowable. Since what is different is feared, the existence of the Other becomes a threat. These beliefs are largely responsible for keeping women subordinated, or confined within their own sphere. Simone de Beauvoir argues that women's being has been defined as Otherness throughout history, and that women and men alike are steeped in this mythology.[5]

In research in this area, Karen Horney has found that much of the suspicion and distrust man feels is understandable because it is based on resentment of capabilities that he does not possess and anxiety over woman's ability to castrate him. His dread of the female is directed against her as a sexual being, and relates to feelings toward his mother which he experienced in his formative years. Women are feared because of their mysterious powers, but are prevented from "real" accomplishments by childbirth and menstruation. Dread, Horney finds, comes from the fear that women can influence the male genital. The man fears that he must surrender his vital strength to her, and that he is more sexually dependent on her than she on him.[6]

Early views of women as different, frightening, threatening, devious, strange, powerful, and dangerous have been perpetuated through myth, religion, philosophy, and cultural belief. Some argue that they have created a basis out of which other forms of oppression were allowed to grow. Because women were pictured in such negative ways, they were excluded from a number of institutions, such as the religious and political, and assigned to others, primarily the family. They were given a distinctive place in the division of labor. Thus, women's minority group status was created and perpetuated, setting up the conditions for developing psychological oppression in the form of self-hatred in women as a group. A woman who accepts an image of herself as the lower or inferior self, the Other, is not likely to develop psychological strength and the motivation to enter new roles. Thus the early views of women as different and unknowable come to be institutionalized and taught to each new generation as part of their world view. The psychological characteristics which result then are often labeled "typically feminine."

DEFENSIVE FEMININE TRAITS

Frustration of their positions can engender in women certain "defensive traits," including self-pity, timidity, silliness, and self-consciousness.[7] A woman's personality cannot be entirely healthy if she has accepted her conditioning about women's sphere and functions. If a woman accepts her traditional role, she may have vague feelings of worthlessness, may lack self confidence, and may be dissatisfied with herself and her life. Often she takes this as her own failure, attributable to some inner fault or lack. A woman is often made aware of her lower prestige, yet she feels that she is a failure if she does not act in accordance with "feminine" expectations.[8] Thus, a woman may feel somewhat inferior according to the standards of success in our society if she acts "womanly," but may feel rejected and "unfeminine" if she does not.

These feelings of worthlessness are often accompanied by a preference for the masculine role and a rejection of the feminine role. Surveys and polls have shown that girls and women are more likely than boys and men to have shown a preference for being a member of the opposite sex.[9] Male babies are preferred to female babies. In general, things that are done by men are evaluated more highly than those done by women.

Others have concluded that women are more likely to display "neurotic" traits as a result of their socialization to feminine roles. Women often become over-sensitive, quick to see slights even when none exist, self-conscious, and somewhat nervous and unstable. Janet Chafetz suggests that "victimized people tend to suffer from a lack of self-confidence, or an inferiority complex."[10] There are a number of "typically female" character traits which grow out of women's oppressed position, including whining, nagging, complaining, sniping, malingering, sabotage, cattiness, touchiness, suspiciousness, and petty attention-getting. "These unattractive postures crop up whenever people are dependent on other individuals in a close, unequal personal relationship."[11]

Other negative psychological characteristics have been explained as being the result of the relatively useless or trivial role of the middle-class woman in American society. Nothing gives people less status than their utter uselessness, and a person is minimized or trivialized by being laughed at.[12] Even though a woman has her own activities and sphere, evaluation is not sufficiently high to provide feelings of genuine usefulness and accomplishment.

> *In an action-oriented, future time-minded society, having no job to do engenders a feeling of uselessness which in turn creates emotional disturbance. Most of us have witnessed the disoriented behavior and emotional stress of women whose children have grown up and gone. Some respond by clinging to children, others try desperately to fit into jobs . . . ; others become unnecessarily fussy housewives; some are merely restless.*[13]

Women are often criticized for their behavior no matter how they act. If they are ambitious, they are criticized for being pushy or bitchy, if not, for lacking drive. "Quiet acceptance, withdrawal from competition and behind-the-scenes fuming are the most common responses among women."[14]

Thus, "feminine" traits, such as passivity, dependency, and inhibition are essentially responses to powerlessness. As Helen Mayer Hacker has explained it, women display the characteristics of self-conscious minority groups, including group self-hatred and accommodation attitudes. These attitudes include using "feminine wiles," flattering and appearing helpless.[15]

BEHAVIORAL OUTCOMES

The oppression of women has been described as producing the character traits which are assumed to be natural to them. In this section, we will discuss in greater detail four major areas in which the effects of this oppression manifest themselves psychologically. These are: (1) motivation to avoid success; (2) the "problem that has no name"; (3) mental and physical illness; and (4) overconcern with youth and beauty.

1. Motivation to Avoid Success

Matina Horner is responsible for a series of studies of college women which have revealed what she terms their "fear of success."[16] Horner began studying this area because she saw bright college women seemingly confused and actually fearful about situations of achievement. Horner believed not that women exhibited a "will to fail," but that they were caught in a double bind where "success" in the achievement sphere might mean failure in the "feminine" sphere. Anxiety about achieving success seemed to result because women expected negative consequences—in the form of social rejection and feelings of being unfeminine—for achievement. Thus, if a woman fails in an achievement-oriented situation, she is not living up to her own standards of performance, but if she succeeds, she is not living up to the societal expectations of the female role.

Horner tested her hypothesis by asking male and female undergraduates to tell a story based on the lead: "After first-term finals, Anne (John) finds herself (himself) at the top of her (his) medical school class." The women wrote about Anne, the men about John. The stories women told were of three types: stories reflecting strong fears of social rejection and anxiety about becoming unpopular; stories reflecting guilt or concern over success and womanhood, doubts about femininity and normality; and stories that completely denied the possibility that a woman could be that successful. Of the 90 women, 65 percent told stories that fell into one of these categories, indicating that they seemed to be troubled or confused over the situation of a woman being at the top of her medical school class. Less than 10 percent of the men showed evidence of a motive to avoid success. Further research indicated most women in her study would explore their intellectual potential most only when they did not need to compete and least when competing with men. Thus, as she points out, legal and educational barriers to female achievement may have been removed, but a psychological barrier remains. Young women still become anxious over the threat of negative consequences, positive achievement strivings become thwarted, and "their abilities, interests, and intellectual potential remain inhibited and unfulfilled."[17]

Horner began her studies in the late 1960s but her more recent research has not shown a lessening of fears of success in women students. The only change has been in the increasingly negative view men students take of success as traditionally defined. On the whole, however, it might be said that men do not exhibit a *fear* of success, but rather a rejection of what success has come to mean. Women were not so much concerned with the rejection of the concept of success as they were with the fear of how they would be regarded if they were successful according to the present definition. This seems to be borne out by studies which show that the "fear of success" is more prevalent among young women in the dating and "courtship" years.[18] Men may show more *fear* of success when the success is in a "feminine" profession,[19] or in other words, when they fear rejection for being deviant. Horner's fear of success refers to women's fear of competing and achieving in a *man's* world, in the "outside world" of work and intellectual pursuits. More recent studies have begun to show equally high levels of "fear of success" for both men and women,[20] and as much success imagery as failure imagery for women.[21] On the whole, the findings are ambiguous. Possibly the anxiety over achieving has lessened for women since Horner began her studies.

2. The Problem That Has No Name

In 1963, Betty Friedan published *The Feminine Mystique,* a book which has been credited with being a major early impetus of the women's movement. Friedan was particularly concerned with a problem of the American middle-class housewife, a problem which was vague almost to the point of being indefinable. It consisted of feelings of frustration, meaninglessness, and lack of fulfillment, but because of the difficulty of pinpointing the source of the problem, Friedan labeled it "the problem that has no name."

Friedan argued that with the end of the Second World War came a return to traditional, almost Victorian attitudes about women staying home to be wives and mothers. The decade of the 1950s became the years of "togetherness," and the period which exalted the home and the "little woman." Friedan felt that the "problem that had no name" arose because the woman was being presented with the image of the happy suburban housewife, but she was finding out that this was not enough. The middle-class housewife was confused and bewildered because she could not understand how her life could seem to be a problem when she had everything she had ever dreamed of having. She simply kept asking herself, "Is this all?" The problem that had no name was emptiness, feeling incomplete, trapped, dissatisfied, unfulfilled, bored, and at times even desperate.

A woman who dared to step out of her "natural role" as wife-mother and have a career was pictured in much of the media of the time as frustrated, masculinized, castrating, and losing her sexuality. The housewife-mother was pictured as "truly feminine," admired by others for her domestic abilities and accomplishments. Even so, the "problem" remained. Although women tried to fill the voids they felt in their lives by having more babies and becoming more and more domestic, these activities failed to provide the solution. The real problem, said Friedan, was one of identity, stunting of intellectual growth, and not permitting women to fulfill their potential as human beings.[22]

Because of the role they were expected to play, women were being shaped into psychologically damaged creatures, when compared with a male or human standard of psychological strength. They were passive, dependent, submissive, weak, self-sacrificing, and on the whole limited. As a result of this narrow restrictive role they were restless and bored, with no sense of personal identity, and little self-esteem despite the glorification of their activities. They suffered from "housewife's syndrome" and sometimes bordered on the neurotic.

3. Mental and Physical Illness

The "problem that has no name" meant that housewives were left feeling bored, frustrated, unfulfilled and anxious. These problems, if they became noticeable, came to be considered signs of mental instability and neuroticism. The syndrome then can be applied to the outward signs of misery that Germaine Greer describes in *The Female Eunuch*.[23] To Greer, these neurotic signs include discontent, apathy, irritability, excessive tiredness, overweight, and premature aging. The neurotic housewife then invents excuses for her irritability and tiredness by claiming illness, pain, headaches, backaches, and inability to sleep. Because she cannot accept her monotonous drudgery and meaningless work as rewarding, she in fact suffers from very real tiredness, lassitude, and "nerves" which are of a complex psychosomatic origin. She thus lapses into hypochondria, or martyrdom and self-righteousness over her ability to carry on in the face of her suffering. She revolts and acts out her discontent and unhappiness in the form of destructive carping and rigidity, and gives vent to her resentment through verbal aggression, reproaches, complaints and petty belittling. However, rather than being helped to escape from her dreary and oppressive prison, she is treated with stimulants, barbituates, or tranquilizers, which have the effect of dulling her misery and resentment, while not improving her mental state.[24]

An important point here is that much of the woman's mental or psychological dysfunction is considered hysterical, exaggerated, or simply not real. There seems to be sexual prejudice against women with regard to alleged psychogenic pain: for example, dysmenorrhea, the nausea of pregnancy, and labor pains.[25] While these problems have very real physical sources, they are often dismissed by the medical establishment as "female" problems of an hysterical sort.

> Our cultural colonization extends not just to sex, but even to illness, and the whole half-articulated world of gynecological complaints. For example, if a woman goes to a doctor complaining of period pains, cystitis, or depression during her menopause, her experience of them will lose itself in male nonexperience of them . . . to persuade her that she can't possibly really feel as ill as she says. Behind the male nonexperience lurks the rationalization that women always exaggerate their complaints. When someone refuses to hear you, you respond by turning up the amplification. . . . When women do this we are regarded blandly as unreasonable, ignorant and hysterical. . . . The political implications of this have been exposed by women's liberation in relation to childbirth, contraception, and abortion. Our lack of control over our own bodies matches the worker's lack of control over production.[26]

On the other hand, women need not be viewed as being at the mercy of their biology and anatomy since there is evidence that dysmenorrhea is learned. No menstrual pain is reported by Arapesh women, who are not taught to expect pain.[27] Elsewhere it has been reported that the degree of recognition and treatment of gynecological problems may be traced to the prevailing definition of being a woman.[28] However, it is a myth too often accepted by medical practitioners that women's complaints are psychosomatic and neurotic in origin. As the Boston Women's Health Book Collective has said, women are often treated as if they are wasting the doctor's time or making waves if they ask questions. The value placed on a woman's health becomes obvious when it is noted that her complaints and requests are shown little respect and often are dismissed as neurotic.[29]

Women on the whole are greater utilizers than men of medical care, see more doctors and dentists, and are admitted in higher numbers to hospitals.[30] This does not mean that women are ill more often, only that they use medical services somewhat more, while men seem to wait longer, for various reasons which seem to be associated with their social roles. Stoll suggests that these reasons include the following: it is "unmanly" to worry about health; women are raised to be more aware of health and health care; obtaining health care is impractical for working men; their special functions (e.g., pregnancy, childbirth) require that women become more likely to fall into the pattern of using medical care; men, because of their somewhat higher use of alcohol and tobacco, wish to avoid being given directions about healthful habits; and women seem to be more sensitive to changes in their bodies.[31] Women consume the largest proportion of health services, and yet they are often treated as if they are overutilizing services with unnecessary complaints. The treatment of a woman perceiving a discomfort (whether psychological or physical) often takes the form of a tranquilizer, a paternalistic or a patronizing attitude that it is "all in her head" or that she is only suffering because she is refusing to derive satisfaction from her feminine role. The oppression of this role may have at least partly produced the psychological symptoms, and these symptoms are used in turn to oppress her further.

According to a number of ways of measuring mental illness, women do suffer from higher rates of mental illness than do men. Women have higher rates of first admissions to private psychiatric hospitals, psychiatric care in general hospitals, psychiatric outpatient care, private outpatient psychiatric care, and symptoms of mental illness (according to community surveys).[32] On the other hand, men have higher rates of admission to state and county hospitals and to VA hospitals. It has been argued, primarily by Phyllis Chesler, that the rather high rate of mental disorder in women does not mean that they are inherently more unstable than men, but that their roles in present day society "drive them crazy."[33] She argues that it is sex-role stereotypes which create mental illness in women. Women are expected to be self-sacrificing, compassionately maternal, dependent and unadventurous, and when they fail to act in this way they may be considered mad. However, Chesler adds that woman's actual objective condition of oppression would make any person display symptoms like depression, paranoia, and feelings of inferiority, which are then defined as mental illness. In other words, woman's devaluation, lack of oppor-

Table 8-1 Distribution of patient care episodes by sex by type of psychiatric facility, United States, 1971.

| | | Inpatient services of: | | | | | Outpatient | |
	Total	State and county hospitals	Private hospitals	VA hospitals	General hospital inpatient psych. services	Community mental health centers	Community mental health centers	Other outpatient psych. services
Both sexes	4,009,506	745,259	97,963	176,800	542,642	130,088	622,906	1,693,848
Males	2,044,576	411,907	39,756	172,433	250,087	59,133	298,985	812,275
Females	1,964,930	333,352	58,207	4,367	292,535	70,955	323,921	881,573

Source: Table 20, U.S. Dept. of HEW, NIMH, Mental Health Statistics, "Utilization of Mental Health Facilities, 1971," Washington, D.C.: Govt. Printing Office, 1973.

tunity, and "slave psychology,"[34] create an unbearable situation which leads to symptoms that become defined as mental illness by male society.

Chesler, supported by research done by Pauline Bart,[35] also suggests that the uselessness of the female role after all her children have left the home (Bart's "empty nest syndrome") contributes to the greater likelihood of such symptoms as depression. Women have been shown to suffer relatively high rates of mental breakdown and depression about the time the last child leaves home. This loss of a primary (if not sole) role with little hope of increased roles in the future, combine with other processes of aging and the menopause to create serious depressive problems. Depression is the most common reason for women to seek psychotherapy, and they suffer from much higher rates of depression than do men.[36]

Table 8-2 Number and percent distribution of patient care episodes by age, sex, and diagnosis, all psychiatric facilities, United States, 1971

	Number	% of all diagnoses	Rate per 100,000 pop.
Depressive disorders:			
Both sexes	615,261	15.4	299.8
Males, all ages	201,222	9.8	201.7
Males, 45–64	78,453	17.7	389.5
Females, all ages	414;039	21.1	392.7
Females, 45–64	127,220	28.6	576.9
Alcohol abuse:			
Both sexes	353,020	8.8	172.0
Males, all ages	283,115	13.8	283.8
Males, 45–64	128,262	28.9	636.8
Females, all ages	69,905	3.5	66.3
Females, 45–64	31,734	7.1	143.9

Source: Table 19, U.S. DHEW, NIMH, Mental Health Statistics, "Utilization of Mental Health Facilities, 1971," Washington, D.C.: Govt. Printing Office, 1973.

Chesler also argues that women comply in their own definitions as mentally ill, and in their own incarceration and treatment. They are willing to commit themselves or view themselves as "sick" because they have been conditioned to think that nonfeminine behavior is bad and unnatural. Women, she says, have been socialized to be help-seeking creatures, to be dependent, to ask for guidance, and not to resist the patient or dependent role as men resist it. Thus, Chesler argues that the oppression of women leads to real distress and unhappiness, and the conditioned female role of help-seeking and distress reporting, along with a double standard of mental health (in which the only way to be healthy is to meet the male standards), produces higher rates of mental illness in women. Acting out the "female" role involves being depressed, incompetent, anxious, and submissive, but rejecting the female role involves being hostile, aggressive, and sexually "overactive."[37]

Gove and Tudor are essentially in agreement with this argument, stressing that it is the married woman specifically who suffers from higher rates of mental illness. They suggest that it is the limitation to the housewife role which is sufficiently frustrating to produce a more negative self-image in women, more depression, more psychophysiologic disorders, and more attempts at suicide. Marital status does not have the same effect on mental problems for men, as it is married men who have the most favorable mental health profile. They feel that it is specifically the contradictions in the roles of married women which produce mental illness,[38] a finding which also has been documented by Jessie Bernard.[39] However, a recent study found depression to be related more to "learned helplessness" than to the role of housewife per se, since working wives were also more depressed than working husbands.[40]

Ehrenreich and English have argued that designating women's medical problems as mental illness is simply one way of ignoring their complaints: "In fact, the tendency of doctors to diagnose our complaints as psychosomatic shows that the medical view of women has not really shifted from 'sick' to 'well'; it has shifted from 'physcially sick' to 'mentally ill.'"[41] Thus, the notion that women are weak or fragile or defective (as they were considered in Victorian times) is perpetuated in the psychiatric view of woman's fundamental defectiveness.[42]

The medical system has become a particular target of feminists who call it a powerful instrument of social control (replacing organized religion as a prime source of sexist ideology) and an enforcer of traditional sex roles. According to this view, medicine does not invent social roles, but interprets them to us as biological destiny.[43] Self help, then, is not proposed as an alternative system of medical care, but as a means of acquiring enough knowledge of one's own body to have effective input into the situation and to confront the ongoing system with the need for change within it.[44] Feminist psychotherapy basically overturns traditional psychotherapy by refusing to accept that the fault lies in the individual, and instead, analyzing how the woman's problem arose as a result of living in a sexist, oppressive society. It rejects traditional approaches and theories and is part consciousness-raising and part problem-solving rather than an attempt to remold the woman's character according to a cultural stereotype or to promote an appropriate definition of the nature of women. Thus, rather than encouraging a woman to subjugate herself and conform to some image of "femininity," feminist psychotherapy would encourage her to see how she has been constrained, repressed, and molded into a role, and to explore new roles.[45]

4. Drive for Youth and Beauty

Perhaps part of the reason that women suffer from neurotic and depressed symptoms is that throughout their lives they are bombarded with artificial standards of beauty which require a great deal of effort but which are difficult, if not impossible, to attain. All women are oppressed by the need to keep up their "front" although the styles and extent of the front change frequently. Every society sets up its own standards of beauty—often rigid, elite and narrow—so that few can ever hope to attain that level of beauty. Although some would argue that today's "natural look" lessens the impact of the beauty standard, this new look has influenced young women in college more than anyone else. The somewhat older standards continue to apply to a great number of women.

Daily media presentations of the cultural ideal of beauty bombard viewers. Models of beauty are everywhere in advertising, and the heroine or woman who wins in the end is almost always pretty. Women are taught that prettiness is of ultimate importance—particularly for catching a man—and that it is attainable through a great deal of effort and transformation. Thus, not only are women taught that to be un-pretty is to have failed to live up to that ideal feminine standard, but also are taught that their natural selves are not pretty and require a good deal of work to attain the appropriate cultural standard of beauty. Because very few are born flawless and beautiful according to the standard, many feel driven to seek out specialists who can help them reduce and remold their bodies; color, cut, and style their hair; show them how to "enhance" their appearance with makeup; help them to dress flatteringly; and even perform surgery to change the shape or size of various body parts, to lift their faces, and to remove "unbeautiful" things like warts or facial hair. In some cases, women actually do themselves physical harm in attempting to look beautiful. The bound feet of the woman of traditional China is the most common example, but also potentially harmful were the tight corsets and girdles once fashionable, the pointed-toe, spike-heeled shoes of recent years, and the habit of overdieting in order to look fashionably thin. Sometimes, too, women have damaged themselves with makeups, dyes, and chemicals which were not safe and which led to burns, rashes, infections, or blindness.

A web of artifice of hairdos, hairsprays, clothes, shoes, undergarments, and makeup mold women into stamped-out images and serve to keep them from participating fully in life while making them apologetic about their natural physical beings. This image is based on the perfect model under artificial circumstances, who looks like no real woman has ever looked. The real woman seems, therefore, unacceptable:

> We must try to resemble perfect plastic objects, so that no one will notice what we really are. In ourselves, we smell bad, shed dandruff, our breath

has an odor, our hair stands up or falls out, we sag or stick out where we shouldn't. We can only fool people into liking us by using products that make us products, too.[46]

As Germaine Greer points out, women are apologetic about their bodies, comparing them to the object of desire presented in the media. They think the parts of their bodies, especially breasts and buttocks, are too large or too small, the wrong shape, or too soft. Arms and legs are too hefty or too skinny, hair is too straight or too curly; but whatever one has, it is not what one wants. A woman is dissatisfied with her body as it is and desires to change herself—not just to adorn herself—but to disguise the real, unacceptable self. This arises, says Greer, from fear of rejection and distaste for her body, and no number of compliments or assurances will ever make her believe that her real self is enough:

> *The universal sway of the feminine stereotype is the single most important factor in male and female woman-hatred. Until woman as she is can drive this plastic specter out of her own and her man's imagination she will continue to apologize and disguise herself.*[47]

Finally, women are kept from participating fully in life because of the restrictions placed on them by the requirements of their dress, hair and makeup. The woman who must constantly worry about her hairdo, her makeup, or her false eyelashes is not likely to engage in much physical activity. Neither is the woman whose skirt length requires vigilance or whose shoes limit her from being able to walk at a pace of more than a ladylike stroll.

Bodies and faces seem to constitute divisive forces between women. Women have anxieties about their attractiveness and appeal partly because of their fear of rejection by men, and partly because they have been taught to be competitive with other women. Many are vain and preoccupied with their looks, waste time on trying to improve them, and expend much emotional energy trying to look better than the other women around them. Sadly, few can ever reach what Firestone called the "beauty Ideal," an elitist ideal which by definition leaves out the majority.[48] Alta has described the feeling of competitiveness very well in her article "Pretty," which points out that one major reason women in a group were lonely and separated and not friendly was that they felt that they were constantly being compared, and were being found less attractive than another woman or women in the group.[49] These fears only increased with age as women became more and more fearful of losing their looks, getting fat, turning grey and becoming wrinkled.

On the whole, women seem to have a poor body image. Knowing how important her body is, and yet having such great doubts about its adequacy, a woman comes to dislike it and wish that she could change her appearance. In an attempt to look "beautiful," women often look artificial and unnatural. Densmore points out that for those who can never be beautiful, self-loathing is the result. Even for those who can achieve the ideal, beauty is not permanent and requires constant vigilance. Admiration of this contrived beauty constitutes admiring an artificial object and not a person.[50] Thus, this beauty ideal or "glamour function" makes her into an object and robs a woman of her self-confidence and identity.

When women complain that they are being viewed as sex objects, they mean that they object to being viewed in terms of primary and secondary sexual characteristics and functions exclusively, without regard to their own personal qualities. Men seem to interpret being seen as sex objects as being attractive to the opposite sex, or "sexy."[51] To women, looks and physical attributes become a commodity to be bartered in exchange for a man, and "women learn early that if you are unlovely, you are unloved."[52] A woman is a sex object whether pretty or plain. Being a sex object means that a woman often *is* how she looks; "to some extent and/or to some people we are never more than our appearances."[53] If plain, she may be laughed at, criticized, or just ignored. Plain women are aware of comments and jokes made about unattractive women, and they know that they are not living up to the "ideal." As a result, many find they cannot love themeselves and are unable to believe anyone else could either.[54]

On the other hand, the attractive woman is a sex object who is treated differently, but in some cases, at least, far less seriously than her plainer sister. If beautiful, a woman is sometimes admired but not listened to nor taken seriously, as manikins are not expected to be smart. Intellect is often considered incompatible with beauty.[55]

Germaine Greer also points out that young and pretty women may delude themselves about the amount of abuse meted out to women because they escape most of it. They sometimes suffer from being considered dumb, but they are not insulted (as the unpretty woman is) for being fat, overly skinny, or muscular and large.[56] In fact, the assignment of the glamour function specifically to women puts them at a great disadvantage because while submitting themselves to indignities and restrictions, they are also handing over to men powerful weapons to be used against them.[57] In other words, by caring so much about personal looks, and investing so much of her ego in her attractiveness, a woman leaves herself open to be hurt by being called homely, ugly or lacking in sex appeal. "Woman as sex object" implies a sex role stereotype which is one-dimensional, dealing only with sexuality or sexual function—a body without a mind.[58] This view does not see women as persons, but degrades them to the level of a jar opener—useful, but having only one purpose. Many women like to be thought of as attractive and/or sexy, as do many men, but neither sex wants to be viewed *only* in terms of a single function.

Anything which makes women feel they cannot meet this "beauty ideal" can be especially oppressive. That is why aging has been so often discussed as a particular problem for women. With the emphasis in American society on youth as well as beauty, the aging person is at a special disadvantage. Women especially must continue to present a youthful image, as an old person can no longer be a successful sex object. The middle-aged, fat or unattractive woman becomes not a person, but a joke. Rose Gladstone says that a woman develops a sense of obsolescence and nonexistence as she grows older and as her daily confrontation with a mirror becomes increasingly traumatic.[59] Bell adds that women lose status as they approach middle age. A woman over 40 feels the growing indifference to her and to her sexuality.[60] She is rarely considered interesting (unless she is an object of curiosity because she is "still" beautiful, as in the unusual case of a Marlene Dietrich). At the same time a woman is losing one of her roles—the role of desirable sex object—she is often facing other role losses as well, including those of mother and housekeeper.

Susan Sontag has analyzed the situation quite thoroughly in her article, "The Double Standard of Aging." She finds that women experience growing older with distaste and even shame, trying to hide their age. While partly because of the cultural emphasis on youth, it is true primarily because women are not accepted as they age. For women, being physically attractive counts more than for men and women become sexually ineligible earlier in life than men do. "Good looks in a man is a bonus, not a psychological necessity for maintaining normal self-esteem."[61] For men, the pressures from aging are not quite so great, because many of the qualities men can develop as they age are rarely valued in women or are less possible for women to develop. Men can develop mental powers, knowledge, skill, success in their professions, autonomy, self control, and satisfaction in their work. Women who have had traditional roles have fewer opportunities to develop these qualities. Women lie about their age, says Sontag, because society made it such a shameful and ridiculous thing to grow old. But every time a woman lies, "she becomes an accomplice in her own underdevelopment as a human being."[62] Sontag adds that the belief that old women are particularly repulsive is deeply imbedded in American culture. Greer also points out that pretty women are never unaware that they are aging, and watch for every sign that they are losing their looks with the greatest anxiety.[63]

The argument is not that there is anything wrong with being attractive, or in wanting to look attractive. What is objectionable is an obsession with one's looks or an overvalue on beauty to such an extent that to be unbeautiful is to be stigmatized. Also objectionable are the false, artificial, inhuman, constricting standards of high fashion, the loss of time required to keep oneself beautiful, the feeling that everything goes downhill after age 25, and the exploitation of women by influencing them to increase their consumption of beauty products and services. Among the negative effects of the emphasis on beauty is the view that intellect mars beauty, or is incompatible with it (although Bersheid and Walster found that the work of attractive people was rated more highly than that of less attractive people[64]). Another negative effect of being judged always by one's appearance is that a woman is damned either way. If she doesn't look good, she is laughed at or criticized for not doing something about herself. Because being called ugly or undesirable is one of the worst things one can say to a woman, so it can be used to destroy women in their fight for equality. According to the detractors, it is "only women who are too homely to keep a man who are mixed up in this Women's Lib stuff." But, on the other hand, a woman who *does* try to look attractive is criticized as being narcissistic, too wrapped up in herself, or spending too much time preparing and primping. Beautiful women often are not taken seriously, but sometimes they are the only ones who can catch men's attention. It is not beauty itself which is oppressive, but the overemphasis placed on it and the unrealistic standards reflected in the media. As oppressive as all the requirements of being beautiful are, even more so is the psychological effect the subscription of these values and beliefs has on women.

CONCLUSION

Psychological oppression in women is perpetuated in mythology and the definition of women as the Other throughout history, and is maintained today through present social institutions and reinforced by the mass media. This oppressive definition of women has created a number of "neurotic" psychological characteristics which tend to be regarded as feminine, and has resulted in certain behavioral outcomes. As C. Wright Mills has said, ". . . when an individual is kept in a situation of inferiority, the fact is that he does become inferior."[65] The conclusion seems to be that we need to understand the dynamics of oppression "so as to change the external realities that have the terrible power to invade and distort our inner reality, to make us less than fully human."[66]

NOTES

1. Adrienne Koch, "Two Cheers for Equality," in *The Potential of Women*, ed. Seymour Farber and Roger H. L. Wilson (New York: McGraw-Hill, 1963), pp. 199–215.

2. Janet Saltzman Chafetz, *Masculine/Feminine or Human?* (Itasca, Ill.: F. E. Peacock, 1974), pp. 151–152; Wolfgang Lederer, *The Fear of Women* (New York: Harvest Books, Harcourt Brace Jovanovich), 1968.

3. Mary A. Ferguson, *Images of Women in Literature* (Boston: Houghton-Mifflin, 1973), p. 15.

4. Wendy Martin, "Seduced and Abandoned in the New World: The Image of Woman in American Fiction," in *Woman in Sexist Society*, ed. Vivian Gornick and Barbara Moran (New York: Basic Books, 1971), pp. 329–346.

5. Simone de Beauvoir, *The Second Sex* (New York: Bantam, 1970).

6. Karen Horney, "Distrust between the Sexes," in *Masculine/Feminine,* ed. Betty Roszak and Theodore Roszak (New York: Harper Colophon Books, 1969), pp. 107–116.

7. Elizabeth Janeway, *Man's World, Woman's Place* (New York: Delta Books, 1971).

8. Nona Glazer-Malbin and Helen Youngelson Waehrer, ed., *Woman in a Man-Made World* (Chicago: Rand McNally, 1972), p. 129.

9. Kirsten Amundsen, *The Silenced Majority* (Englewood Cliffs, N.J.: Prentice-Hall, 1971), p. 120, cites a study of fourth-graders which showed ten times as many girls wishing to be boys as boys wishing to be girls. Helen Mayer Hacker, "Woman as a Minority Group," *Social Forces* 30 (1951), pp. 60–69, cites a *Fortune* poll which showed 25% of women wishing they had been born men. Amundsen, 1971, op. cit., p. 122. See also Amitai Etzioni, "Sex Control, Science, and Society," *Science* 161 (September 1968), pp. 1107–1112.

10. Chafetz, op. cit., p. 122.

11. Caroline Bird, *Born Female* (New York: Pocket Books, 1971), p. 194.

12. Morton Hunt, "The Direction of Female Evolution," in Farber and Wilson, op. cit., pp. 255–272.

13. Florence Kluckhohn, "American Women and American Values," in *Facing the Future's Risks,* ed. Lyman Bryson (New York: Harper and Bros., 1953), p. 195.

14. Amundsen, op. cit., p. 4.

15. Hacker, op. cit.

16. Matina Horner, "Toward an Understanding of Achievement-Related Conflicts in Women," *Journal of Social Issues* 28 (1972), pp. 157–175.

17. Ibid., p. 171.

18. M. Kimball, "Women and Success—a Basic Conflict?" in *Women in Canada,* ed. M. Stevenson (Toronto: New Press, 1973).

19. David Tresemer, "Fear of Success: Popular but Unproven," in *The Female Experience, Psychology Today* (1973), pp. 58–62.

20. Marlaine E. Lockheed, "Female Motive to Avoid Success: A Psychological Barrier or a Response to Deviancy?" *Sex Roles* 1 (March 1975), pp. 41–50.

21. T. G. Alper, "Role Orientation in Women," *Journal of Personality* 41 (1973), pp. 9–31.

22. Betty Friedan, *The Feminine Mystique* (New York: Dell, 1963).

23. Germaine Greer, *The Female Eunuch* (New York: Bantam, 1972), p. 290.

24. Ibid.

25. K. Jean Lennane and R. John Lennane, "Alleged Psychogenic Disorders in Women—a Possible Manifestation of Sexual Prejudice," *New England Journal of Medicine* (8 February 1973), pp. 288–292.

26. Sheila Rowbotham, *Woman's Consciousness, Man's World* (New York: Penguin, 1973), p. 37. Copyright © Sheila Rowbotham, 1973. Reprinted by permission of Penguin Books Ltd.

27. Margaret Mead, *Male and Female* (New York: Dell, 1949).

28. Irving K. Zola, "Culture and Symptoms—an Analysis of Patients' Presenting Complaints," in *Medical Men and Their Work,* ed. Eliot Freidson and Judith Lorber (New York: Aldine-Atherton, 1972).

29. The Boston Women's Health Book Collective, *Our Bodies, Ourselves* (New York: Simon and Schuster, 1971, 1973).

30. There are many studies in this area. For a thorough review, see Lu Ann Aday, Research Associate, and Robert L. Eichhorn, Director, *The Utilization of Health Services: Indices and Correlates, A Research Bibliography,* Health Services Research and Training Program, Dept. of Sociology, Purdue Univ., Lafayette, Ind., 1972.

31. Clarice Stasz Stoll, *Female and Male: Socialization, Social Roles, and Social Structure* (Dubuque, Iowa: Wm. C. Brown Co., 1974).

32. Walter R. Gove and Jeannette F. Tudor, "Adult Sex Roles and Mental Illness," *American Journal of Sociology* 78 (January 1973), pp. 50–73.

33. Phyllis Chesler, *Women and Madness* (New York: Doubleday, 1972).

34. Thomas Szasz, *The Myth of Mental Illness* (New York: Delta Books, 1961).

35. Pauline Bart, "Depression in Middle-Aged Women," in Gornick and Moran, op. cit., pp. 163–186.

36. Chesler, op. cit., citing NIMH statistics, p. 41.

37. Chesler, op. cit.

38. Gove and Tudor, op. cit.

39. Jessie Bernard, *The Future of Marriage* (New York: Bantam, 1973).

40. Lenore Radloff, "Sex Differences in Depression: The Effect of Occupation and Marital Status," *Sex Roles* 1 (September 1975), pp. 249–265.

41. Barbara Ehrenreich and Deirdre English, *Complaints and Disorders, Glass Mountain Pamphlet #2* (Old Westbury, N.Y.: The Feminist Press, 1973), p. 79.

42. Ibid.

43. Ibid., p. 83.

44. See Ehrenreich and English, op. cit.; Ellen Frankfort, *Vaginal Politics* (New York: Quadrangle Books, 1972).

45. See, for instance, Anica Vesel Mander and Anne Kent Rush, *Feminism as Therapy* (New York: Random House; Berkeley: Bookworks, 1974).

46. Zoe Moss, "It Hurts To Be Alive and Obsolete: The Aging Woman," in *Sisterhood is Powerful,* ed. Robin Morgan (New York: Vintage, 1970), p. 170.

47. Greer, op. cit., p. 277.

48. Shulamith Firestone, *The Dialectic of Sex* (New York: Bantam, 1970).

49. Alta, "Pretty," in Gornick and Moran, op. cit., pp. 35–36.

50. Dana Densmore, "On the Temptation To Be a Beautiful Object," in *Toward a Sociology of Women,* ed. Constantina Safilios-Rothschild (Lexington, Mass.: Xerox College Publishing, 1972), pp. 96–99; Jessie Bernard, *Women and the Public Interest* (Chicago: Aldine-Atherton, 1971).

51. For this conclusion I am indebted to Mark Krain, who devised a questionnaire which he administered to his own class and which I administered to mine. The differing interpretations of the meaning of "sex object" came out in discussions with my class.

52. Una Stannard, "The Mask of Beauty," in Gornick and Moran, op. cit., p. 195.

53. Densmore, op. cit., p. 98.

54. Stannard, op. cit.

55. Densmore, op. cit.

56. Greer, op. cit.

57. Bernard, op. cit.

58. Sandra Shevy, "Down with Myth America," in *The Other Half,* ed. Cynthia F. Epstein and William J. Goode (Englewood Cliffs, N.J.: Spectrum (Prentice-Hall), 1971), pp. 62–64.

59. Rose Gladstone, "Planned Obsolescence: The Middle-Aged Woman," in *Liberation Now!,* ed. Deborah Babcox and Madeline Belkin (New York: Dell, 1971), pp. 145–149.

60. Inge Powell Bell, "The Double Standard: Age," in *Women: A Feminist Perspective,* ed. Jo Freeman (Palo Alto, Calif.: Mayfield, 1975).

61. Susan Sontag, "The Double Standard of Aging," *Saturday Review,* 23 September 1972, p. 36.

62. Ibid., p. 38.

63. Greer, op. cit.

64. Ellen Berscheid and Elaine Walster, "Beauty and the Best," *Psychology Today,* (March 1972).

65. C. Wright Mills, "Women: The Darling Little Slaves," in *Power, Politics, and People,* ed. Irving Louis Horowitz (New York: Ballantine, 1963), p. 343.

66. Barbara Grizutti Harrison, *Unlearning the Lie: Sexism in School* (New York: Liveright Publishing Corporation, 1973), p. 174.

ADDITIONAL REFERENCES

1. Bernard, Jessie. *Women and the Public Interest.* Chicago: Aldine-Atherton, 1971.

2. Etzioni, Amitai. "Sex Control, Science, and Society." *Science* 161, September 1968, pp. 1107–1112.

3. Lederer, Wolfgang. *The Fear of Women.* New York: Harvest Books, Harcourt Brace Jovanovich, 1968.

4. Lynn, David. "The Process of Learning Parental and Sex-Role Identification." *Journal of Marriage and Family* 28, 1966, pp. 446–470.

9
THE WOMEN'S MOVEMENT

A woman without a man is like a fish without a bicycle.

—*People Weekly*

ORIGINS OF THE MOVEMENT

After the passage in 1920 of the Nineteenth Amendment, granting women suffrage, interest in feminism as a cause declined. However, social events of the next decades increased the renewed questioning of women's traditional roles. In a period of increasing industrialization, rising affluence, and concern over population control, women came to assume an ever more important part in the labor force at the same time that improved contraception methods enabled them to control child bearing. Although the 1950s was a period when fertility was encouraged, "the dream of happiness in suburbia was turning sour,"[1] and women began to turn away from the family in search of meaningful work. Finally, the growing civil rights movement of the early 1960s began to call into question traditional ideologies and open the way for the ideology of the New Left. Working women, housewives, and students all began to question the status quo and to reformulate the feminist ideology.

From *People Weekly* Magazine, July 26, 1976, p. 20.

Broad social changes, including increased urbanization and mobility, rapid modernization, technological development,[2] and changes in rates of mortality, fertility, and migration influenced the structure of the family and contributed to the changed status of women.[3] However, rather than the changes in society resulting in equal status for women and men, women were granted a sort of quasi-egalitarianism, resulting in tokenism and enhancing women's influence in increasingly obsolete spheres. The discovery that the ideology was egalitarian while the reality was not led to self-reflection and eventual awareness of the inequities.[4]

Within an environment of social change, protest, and rising awareness, women began to become active in their own behalf. One of the two major sources of the present women's movement was the interest in women's rights begun in the early 1960s. In 1961, President Kennedy created the President's Commission on the Status of Women. This commission brought together politically active women, produced evidence of women's unequal status and created the expectation that something would be done about the inequities found. Soon after this, in 1963, the release of Betty Friedan's *The Feminine Mystique* added to the growing ranks of feminists many thousands of women who could understand "the problem that had no name." The following year the word "sex" was added to the Civil Rights Act of 1964, thus barring discrimination on the basis of sex along with race, religion, and national origin. Out of the interest generated by these events, the National Organization for Women was formed on June 30, 1966, with Betty Friedan heading the effort. The membership of NOW was small, but because the members were successful at securing media coverage, their activities assumed an importance in the public mind they might not have had without this wide exposure.

A later impetus to the movement sprang from different causes. It is generally believed that women in this later, more radical, arm of the movement, were originally women who were involved with the New Left, protests, civil rights, and peace activities. Through their participation in these activities, women developed many of the organizational skills needed to organize on their own, as well as the degree of consciousness and militancy necessary to challenge male leadership. Besides being ignored, being expected to do the "female" tasks (such as making coffee, typing, and so on), and being considered as little more than movement "groupies," women were also sometimes ridiculed and insulted when attempting to be heard. At a SNCC (Student Non-Violent Coordinating Committee) meeting in 1964, Ruby Doris Smith Robinson presented a paper titled, "The Position of Women in SNCC." It was this paper which elicited Stokely Carmichael's comment, "The only position for women in SNCC is prone." Women began to come together and discuss the irony of the fact that the price for participation in a battle for someone else's equality was the loss of their own. Finally, in 1967, at a Chicago conference (National Conference for a New Politics), two women tried to insert a strong women's rights plank, but were told that their "trivial" business was not going to stop the conference from dealing with the important issues of the world. These two women, Jo Freeman and Shulamith Firestone, went on to found the first radical feminist groups in Chicago and New York and to become important movement theorists and analysts.[5]

By 1968, the activities by and for women were being called "a movement" by the media. The earlier group concentrated on women's rights, and worked through traditional channels. The later group worked for women's libration, or freedom from stereotypes and restrictive roles, and did not work through formal structures at all. Their emphasis was on changing social realities rather than assimilating and adapting to present reality.[6]

ORGANIZATION AND TACTICS

Separate approaches to women's issues require different types of organization and tactics. These differences need not necessarily be viewed as a division from within the movement, but could be viewed as a complementary approach in which some persons work for legal and political changes, others for changes of attitudes, beliefs, and values. Both are necessary, and one style is more suited to certain women than the other. The two thrusts often have been considered to be opposed because those of the reform movement tend to have as a goal giving women the opportunity to compete in the world of men without changing the world. Those of the radical movement are not interested in sharing man's world as it is now but in eradicating sex roles and re-evaluating male standards.

The emphasis on working through channels versus working to overturn the existing system is reflected in the types of structures of the two arms of the movement. The older, reform movement is hierarchical with elected offices, rules of order, and bureaucratic procedures. Organizations of this type have attracted a wide membership which includes male members, and have had some success in dealing with the overt symptoms of sexism, such as legal inequities and employment discrimination. Despite certain successes, this reform type of group with its hierarchical structure has been accused of inhibiting the development of other members.[7] For radical feminists, women's oppression rests in sex-role segregation and power distinctions. Since the philosophy of the radical group is that working through the system is useless, the aim is to make women become more aware of their own oppression and to realize that they are not necessarily to blame for it, but that their condition is a result of continual pressure from a "sexist society." Radical feminists, in wishing to overturn existing arrangements, are committed to ideals of equal participation, internal democracy and an egalitarian non-hierarchical structure.

Rather than working through channels, radical feminists chose to attempt to change women's outlooks through small groups using the techniques of consciousness-raising.[8] Consciousness-raising (CR) meant awakening to one's condition, but also referred to the process of finding courage and confidence to move and to develop a positive self-image. CR has sought to communicate that what a woman traditionally had taken to be a personal problem—and thus her fault—is a political problem and is determined by her position in the social structure.[9] Consciousness-raising sessions and working toward personal liberation serve a resocializing function in that the individual's view of reality is changed. The objective of CR groups is to demonstrate to women that their problems are not unique and that by sharing their experiences they can help each other to better understand their own life situations. Women are urged to speak subjectively and specifically about personal experiences and feelings rather than about abstractions. Through the process women become aware of themselves as individuals and discover the problems which they share simply because they are women. The philosophy of CR is that women's oppression is a collective problem and requires a collective solution.

The gains made through the technique of consciousness-raising cannot really be compared to the gains made by formal organizations working for legislative change. Both are important, though experts disagree on whether a change of stereotyped images or institutional change is more important. "While it is true that the right imagery will help women achieve their due share and status, it is also true that one of the best ways to correct images is to correct the reality."[10] Furthermore, it has been argued that the structurelessness and leaderlessness of the radical groups may lead to self-analysis but not to action with the result that, eventually, the groups will disintegrate. It is possible for structureless groups to turn inward to the extent that they reject everyone who does not entirely agree with their philosophy. However, the idea behind CR was that a mass liberation movement would develop as more and more women began to perceive their situations in this new light, and to recognize their own contained resentment. The basic notion is that change can come about only through recognition of the need for change.

With the help of the mass media, much of the ideology of women's liberation groups has been communicated to vast numbers of people and has drawn increasing numbers of adherents. Discussion and exploration of feminist issues in CR groups tend to have the effect of raising a woman's opinion of other women, and contributing to a "feeling of sisterhood," as well as leading to a consideration of the meaning of liberation for all people. At the same time, group support helps the individual to develop her own feelings of self-respect, self-reliance, self-direction, and autonomy. As Jo Freeman has said, the experience of consciousness-raising is irreversible and contagious; one's view of the world is never the same again and one is almost compelled to tell others of her/his experience.[11]

There have been organizations and tactics of different types, some working for legal and economic changes, others for changes in stereotypes and self-concepts. The latter type seems to have discovered an effective technique for changing individual attitudes but not for effectively dealing with social institutions. The other "reform-oriented" groups have been more politically effective.[12] Structurelessness and hierarchical organization both have their limitations. Both types of organizations and tactics are valuable and necessary, and, as long as they are not in competition, can complement each other.

ISSUES AND GOALS

Not all women who would identify themselves with a women's movement would agree on basic issues, causes of oppression, or goals to be achieved. One group sees the root cause of oppression in economic exploitation, and suggests that women's liberation is part of a worldwide struggle of all exploited people against more powerful classes:

> *Radical women feel an analysis of our economic system shows that sex, race and class discrimination are* necessary *to maintain the control over wealth and resources by the ruling classes and that the role of women will not basically change until there is a radical reorganization of power in America.*[13]

This analysis would indict the capitalist system, suggesting that women are exploited both as a surplus labor force which is channeled back into the home when not needed, and as consumers of the products produced in a capitalist system. Benston suggests that the material basis for discrimination against woman lies in the fact that her work is done privately in the home and is unpaid. Only when homemaking tasks are moved into the public sector will discrimination against women end.[14] Built into this Marxist analysis is the notion that the exploitation of women, the enslavement of women by men, was the original form of class oppression of one group by another and set the pattern for all other forms of oppression which followed.[15] The equalization of women would come through emancipation from private domestic labor and their participation in production on a large scale.[16] However, it has not been found to be true that socialist countries have eradicated sexism, nor that industrializing housework (such as in Israel) has ensured equality of the sexes.

Another group within the movement is less interested in the economic basis of oppression than in the power struggle between men and women; it sees the oppressor not as the capitalist system but as men. Women in this group are basically separatist, often lesbian, and may or may not be man-hating. Some see men as the enemy, while others view men as simply irrelevant, but both would exclude men both as an expression of their anger against oppression by men and as a tactical necessity to enable women to develop their own autonomy. The belief of such groups is that the male-female role system is at the core of all systems of oppression and must be destroyed, and that women must be freed from men.[17]

The logical extreme of freedom from men and changing women's relationship to other women is lesbianism. As Abbott and Love have pointed out ". . . Lesbians provide an example of Feminist theory in action,"[18] as they free themselves from confining sex roles, develop independence and self-determination, and refuse to be sex-objects dominated by men. But besides being a protest against male dominance and an expression of freedom from the restrictions of the feminine role, lesbianism can be seen as an expression of the appreciation of women and femaleness.[19] Lesbianism can be a separatist, alternative life-style for women rejecting male oppression, or it can involve a process of self-discovery and self-affirmation, learning how to relate to another human being as an equal in a mutual, shared relationship.[20]

Depending on which branch of the movement she identifies with, a woman may feel that other women are selling-out or being bought off with token changes, or dividing women by rejecting those who are happy in traditional roles.[21] Some feel the women's movement is only a fad which takes attention away from the more pressing problems of black liberation.[22] The movement has been accused variously of being irrelevant to black and lower-class women; of focusing on bored housewives reacting to their lack of fulfillment; of being over-concerned with aggressive professional women desiring higher status and earnings; of appealing only to students ready for a new cause; and of being designed for man-haters wanting to hold power over men. By defining the movement only in particular ways it has been made to seem to apply to the few rather than to the many. The view that the movement is not for poor or working class women narrowly defines it. In its broadest sense, the movement is concerned not only with women in professions or with getting women out of kitchens, but in seeking a far-reaching idea of change—a change of identity. Thus, what the movement aims to do is to change woman's image as an inferior or secondary creature in the position of serving her superiors. The low-paid working woman suffers as much as anyone else and more than many from being considered a member of a servant class. She is expected to devote her energies to low status jobs and to a family and is paid less than men for her work at the same time.

Therefore, despite the large number of issues which seem to divide women, there remains a central core which might be thought of as the ideology of the movement, on which it could be said that feminist women are agreed. This core has to do with the belief in the existence of sexism and in the importance of freedom from oppression through structural and personal change. Stoll has said that the common denominator among feminists is the belief that women are oppressed, but the reasons for it, the ways it affects women, and the means for ending it are open to question. There is agreement within the movement that there is social and economic discrimination, and that change is needed, but there is little agreement beyond that because the movement has existed as a conglomeration of special interest groups devoted to improving the status of women.[23] Freeman finds that there are two theoretical concerns in the interpretation of women's status on which everyone agrees: the feminist critique of a society which has assumed that men and women were unequal, with entirely different capabilities; and the notion of sexism, which emphasizes that men are more important than women and women are expected to support and assist men.[24] The eradication of sexism and sexist practices is the most basic goal of the women's movement. There seems to be fairly widespread agreement within the *movement* on the idea of freedom from oppression and arbitrary limits, and on emphasis on increasing alternatives for both sexes, although obviously not all *women* in America believe that women are oppressed.

In more specific terms, there is a certain amount of agreement on particular issues including equalizing legal rights; eliminating economic and employment discrimination; granting women rights to and control over their own bodies; and increasing political power. There is also some agreement on certain broader and more amorphous goals: to reduce and eliminate stereotyping, particularly in the mass media; to reduce the need for artifice and increase the value of naturalness; to be able to pursue alternatives without stigma; to be willing to accept greater responsibility along with greater rights and freedoms; and to develop a sense of history, solidarity and sisterhood. Feminist women hope to improve their own self-images, and they hope to increase women's opinions of women as a group. Once a feeling of self-regard and sisterhood is attained, women are more able to consider the meaning of liberation for all people. Most women need to develop their own selves to the point where they do not have to defer to males, for only then can they begin to see their brothers as oppressed as well.

In spite of fairly widespread agreement on such goals as independence and freedom, there can be negative implications of these goals as well. The overemphasis on independence can lead to developing a reserve and a distance to the point that warm interpersonal relationships are no longer possible. Freedom of choice for women may mean only that women will have greater opportunities to be pressured to pursue goals which have driven men to illness and early death.[25] There is a distinct possibility that the woman allowed to enter the competitive, achievement-oriented world of men will find only that the situation was not what she wanted at all. Again the answer seems to be in recognizing which societal values are worth pursuing, and which need to be modified.

Efforts should be in the direction of re-structuring institutions and eliminating the dual system of values. This would be accomplished not by eliminating "feminine" values and assimilating women into the world of "masculine" values, but by re-evaluating the value system as a whole and modifying it. Narrowly defined, a "women's movement" could have the effect of "freeing" everyone for the maximum pursuit of individual goals, being accompanied by the destruction of personal relationships, normlessness, and alienation. The question of whether the women's movement will result in alienation or in a more humane society[26] cannot be answered because the ultimate direction of the movement has yet to be determined. However, the increasing concern seems to be in promoting human liberation, rather than the liberation of women from the oppression of men.

In reviewing Simone de Beauvoir's *The Second Sex*, C. Wright Mills stated that he felt that the condition of women was being confused with the generic human condition, in that while women were not allowed a life of accomplishment, or freedom to shape either their destinies or the concept of femininity and masculinity, the same could be said of men. Mills also pointed to the exploitative parasite, the manipulative woman, and the woman who used sex as a tool of power to show that it is not always women who are exploited. His suggestion was to completely remake both sexes and allow members of each to be equally free to become independent human beings.[27]

Others writing more recently than Mills have also suggested that both sexes should be "remade." Alice Rossi would aim at a radical reassignment of functions, so that change could come not only from women but from men. Her hybrid model implies a total eradication of sex role stereotypes and division of labor based on sex. This view proposes that since not all would *want* to adopt male values and standards, the goal is not to make women more like men, but to make all people more human.[28]

Roxanne Dunbar has said that women must assert feminism as a positive force rather than asking for equality in a man's world, and women must demand that men change.[29] Better yet, women's task is to show men how it is to their advantage to change. Women must be sincere about accepting responsibility and about refusing to exploit men if they expect men to see any advantages to sharing their own rights and power. Persons of both sexes who are solidly entrenched in their roles see changes as destructive. The constructive side of human liberation needs to be presented more fully and convincingly.

FEMINISM AS A SOCIAL MOVEMENT
According to Amitai Etzioni, the women's movement has made it as far as recognition is concerned.[30] Selected findings from a national

survey on public attitudes toward the family conducted in 1972 and 1973 revealed that 55 percent of all adults surveyed reported that they were "completely for" the women's movement or "more for than against" it (58 percent of men and 51 percent of women). This was an increase from 49 percent in favor in 1972 (54 percent of men, 44 percent of women). Of four "liberal movements," it was the only one which received a significant rise in support. Attitudes were more favorable the younger the respondent.[31] However, there is not complete agreement at this point that the women's movement can be called a social movement at all. Helen Dudar, for instance, has said that it is doomed to being a fad if it does not develop sufficient structure, organization, and mass membership.[32] Barbara Polk has suggested that the movement has been relatively ineffective because of the lack of organization and clear goals.[33] However, Kirsten Amundsen suggests that it can become a broadly based and potent social movement because its basis for unity is the aim to end institutionalized oppression of women, a goal which involves all women.[34]

Kyriakos Kontopoulos has found that the events of the 1960s marked the transition from a "general amorphous" to a "general instituted" stage of the movement. The events referred to included a radical search for identity through other action groups; a literary articulation by writers (such as Friedan, de Beauvoir and Mead); and the creation of neo-feminist groups. He considers the movement still general and hesitating, rather than full-blown, because of its lack of internal unity, specifically articulated ideology, and organization. A final drawback is its lack of ability to include other women besides "professionals, students, and intellectuals." Kontopoulos concludes that the movement most needs an appropriate ideological position, which he feels is the belief in human liberation from sociocultural pressures and sexist institutions.[35]

Disagreeing with Kontopoulos, Chafetz finds that women's liberation is a full-blown social movement, based on Smelser's stages of social movements which involve the presence of social strain, anxiety, attribution of the strain to certain agents, and belief that value changes will destroy or restrict the responsible agents and result in a new and better society. She, too, notes the ineffectiveness of organizational looseness in striving for concrete, normative changes, but feels that both a non-organizational and a more structured approach exist within the movement and together can effect change.[36]

In another analysis of the movement, Jo Freeman has demonstrated that the women's movement developed as a movement because of a preexisting communication network which was co-optable because of its receptivity to the ideas of the incipient movement. Crises were needed to galvanize activity, and subsequent organizational efforts welded the spontaneous groups—diversified within but working toward common goals—into a movement.[37] Glenda Sehested has suggested that this process works through a reconstruction of social reality. According to her analysis, feelings of relative deprivation result in a movement when a group of persons sharing a common structural position interact with each other: "The origins of the women's movement lie in the collective reconstruction of the reality of the 'place' of women in society."[38] The communications media play a large part in this process of allowing persons to observe others in their own position. Thus, through becoming aware of one's similarities to others in similar circumstances, one's consciousness is raised, and a new reality constructed. Sehested points out, however, that although the development of a systematic ideology is important, premature crystalization of the ideology runs the risk of attaining short-term goals at the expense of long-run ones. Both Etzioni and Chafetz warn that the movement runs the risk of being bought off by token changes, not because ideology has prematurely crystallized, but because movement women may emphasize superficial changes and end with no real improvement at all.

Etzioni believes that there are certain factors which favor the future success of women's liberation and points out that the fate of popular movements is often determined by historical forces the movement cannot control. The factors favoring women's liberation include the acceptance of birth control techniques, the automation of household services, the spread of college education, the heightening of political awareness, the increasing concern for the quality of life and the fact that the potential base of the movement is the majority of the population.[39] This, however, does not suggest what final form the movement will take.

An important thrust of the women's movement has been the rejection of a monolithic organization of leadership and power, and of a single ideology. Most social scientists seem to agree that with such beliefs the movement cannot succeed, but that it *will* need leaders, organization, and a single ideology. Many also seem to feel that the present stage is one of preparation for the long haul, of working out solutions to problems of definition, strategy, tactics, communication, means, and ends.

Strategies must include articulating a broad interpretation of the movement so as to include more people and to avoid rejecting others. The strategy will include using a positive approach which demonstrates benefits, rather than using a hostile approach which frightens or threatens and in the long run is non-productive. A closer alliance with male liberation is required, as all people potentially could agree on basic goals of desiring freedom from oppression, greater choice and options in deciding their own fates, and greater tolerance and acceptance of varying life styles, with consequent changes in values about what is unacceptable, deviant, or stigmatized.

The future of the movement is dependent on several things, including the continued and increased interest of women and men in the issues (as it could be defeated by apathy); the possibility of a backlash; the failure to incorporate women of various classes and backgrounds; and the narrowness of its goals and inability to appeal to men. Almost all writers on the subject seem to feel that the movement is more likely to succeed if the true goals are human liberation.

What, then, of the future? What can be expected if the movement is a success? We may expect to see changes in the institutions toward greater equality in participation in all spheres; we may expect to see changes in cultural values, away from the "male standard" and in the direction of what might be considered "humane" values; we may see changes in the image of women, and probably the emergence of a new "ideal" woman who is neither earth mother nor sex-goddess but a warm, competent, autonomous human being; and we would expect similar changes in the roles and images of men. In other words, what happens to the women's liberation movement or to the human liberation movement depends on the development of a new ideology, the redefinition and reconstruction of reality. A new reality will result from talking about and exploring the old reality, with the hope that the new one will be more appropriate to our needs.

CONCLUSION

Neither this chapter nor this book should be viewed as a blueprint for the future. It is intended as an exploration of the status quo and its implications for (or effects on) the behaviors and psychology of women. It is not the task of the sociologist to suggest societal changes, but to provide an analysis of social events which can help to predict the outcome of events. From the available evidence, we should be able to reach some tentative conclusions.

First, it is obvious that the women's movement, whether officially a social movement or not, has not proved to be merely a passing fad. It has gained adherents and a certain amount of respectability in the eyes of the public. This movement grew out of objective conditions of oppression against women, combined with the rising awareness of their deprivation, and has been promoted through efficient and far-reaching media of mass communication.

Part of the reason for the "success" of the movement may well be its internal divisions. Although this may sound contradictory, the fact is that the "radical" sector seems to have done its part in raising consciousness, while the more conservative sector has worked effectively for legal and political changes. Both are important and necessary, and so long as one does not denounce the other, both can work in a complementary manner. Despite differences in goals, techniques, theoretical views, organization, and operational styles, all members of the women's movement have found themselves to be united on the simple goals of liberation and freedom from oppression.

The question of whether women or men are more oppressed cannot be easily settled as there are ways in which each sex is oppressed which the other will never experience. The women's and men's movements for liberation are not in competition with each other. This book has been more concerned with how women have been (and continue to be) systematically excluded from those areas of life considered to be most important according to dominant cultural values. Whether or not these values—achievement, success, activism, individualism, and so on— are the "best" ones for a society is not the issue here. Our purpose has been to analyze the present situation of women in America in order to determine whether or not they could be said to be "oppressed" in the sense of being held back from full participation. The facts speak for themselves and this clearly seems to be the case. The choices, then, are these: this system can continue, and be accepted as right and natural; the movement toward women's liberation can insist that women become an integral part of society and the equals of men; or the movement toward human liberation can work for a modification of cultural values and a change in sex role expectations, so that requirements for "success" are defined much more flexibly and role requirements are not bound by sex.

Advocates of the human liberation approach remind us that there are severe restrictions on both sexes, all of which are arbitrary in the sense that they are imposed because a person is born either female or male, and not because she or he is suited for a role. Men's roles have higher status in our society, but in many ways they are more restricted. Women, at least, may take part in many of men's activities, but ridicule and loss of status keep almost all men from entering so-called "feminine" areas of interest. In a physical or geographical sense, men seem to have more freedom, but in an attitudinal and behavioral sense (especially where there may be implications in their behavior of homosexuality) men may be far more limited.[40] Thus we can only repeat: the women's movement and the men's movement are not in competition but are two sides of the same coin. Both are seeking freedom from arbitrary restrictions and stereotyping; both are interested in a truer sharing between people; both are asking for a greater variety of alternatives and greater freedom to choose. Both are, of course, asking for change.

Can we predict the course of the movement for human liberation? As a movement, we have seen how it can build its strength. It appears that it is through changing the social definitions of reality that change will come. We can continue to change this social definition through consciousness-raising for both men and women and through formal courses and lectures. We can see to it that women attain positions of power and responsibility, and can then act as role models and help to change negative attitudes about what women can accomplish. We can also attempt to change one major source of much information and a great many of our stereotypes by attempting to influence presentations in the mass media—newspapers, television, magazines, movies, and books. The mass media are vitally important as a major potential source of changing our collective definition of reality. For example, newspapers have contributed to improving attitudes toward women's liberation, as women's issues are now being treated more seriously, and "women's pages" are no longer exclusively devoted to wedding announcements, recipes and sewing hints.

In a discussion of the women's movement, it should be remembered that most women are not connected in any formal way with any group or organization which might define itself as part of the movement. Therefore, to speak of women's liberation, or even more broadly of human liberation, is potentially to include almost everyone. The fact is that the women's liberation movement is not a movement, as Caroline Bird says, but a state of mind: "The secret strength of the Movement is that this state of mind propagates itself by contagion."[41] However, despite the apparent benefits for society, many people feel they have nothing to gain and much to lose. In addition to the women who have felt rejected by the movement, men have felt threatened by their potential losses. To many it has seemed not that women were asking for a more humane and equitable and less competitive society, but were demanding power to assume men's status and prestige and replace them at the top of the hierarchy. This fear may be attributable to lack of communication more than to any real threat, as most movement women are in no way interested in "depriving men of their manhood" or in relegating them to inferior positions. Women have, however, questioned why they should be deprived of those very rights and privileges which define "manhood" for men: initiative, responsibility, self-respect, and being taken seriously. Perhaps it could be more simply stated that depriving anyone of these rights in American society is depriving them of their humanness.

Some stand to lose something if the movement for human liberation should define the future. Anyone who has held absolute authority on the basis of an arbitrary distinction could well lose much of his (or her) power. However, the potential for positive action seems much greater than the threat. The direction that the movement takes from here cannot be predicted. It probably will be based on ideological decisions which will be related to societal conditions such as birth rate and population problems, the economy and the need for labor, the development of technology and so on. Whatever the future goals may be, it seems increasingly obvious that true liberation for all people can result only if two ethics—referred to as the Egalitarian and the Liberation ethics by Jo Freeman—continue to develop. The Egalitarian Ethic says that sex roles must go because the sexes are equal, but the Liberation Ethic takes this one step further and says that not only must the limits of the roles be changed, but the content as well, because both the masculine and feminine roles as presently defined are deplorable. The two Ethics, says Freeman, must work in tandem, because equality without liberation frees no one, and liberation through equality (for example, under socialism) has by no means eliminated sexism.[42]

Thus, while the future is not known, it can be suggested that the success of a movement toward liberation for all people requires a recognition of the different sorts of oppression. It can be only destructive to launch a movement based on hate and divisiveness, to insist on blaming one whole group of persons or alienating potential members, to threaten or use power to hurt. It is also not useful to turn inward to the point of non-communication with outsiders, unless the aim is to keep the movement small and contained. If, however, the purpose of the movement is to convert all people and change the collective definition of reality, the best approach is to appeal on the basis of advantages for everyone. Freedom has its drawbacks in insecurity and anxiety, and it is not uncommon for people to escape from freedom by plunging into authoritarianism, destructiveness, or automaton conformity.[43] However, the freedom we enjoy is always limited by the agents of social control and our own internalization of those controls. Our freedom lies in recognizing those constraints and limits and then dealing with them with strength and sensitivity. The challenge of the liberation movement is to become aware and then to deal with this new awareness. It is a challenge, not just to special interest groups, but to all humanity.

NOTES

1. Marlene Dixon, "Why Women's Liberation?" in *Liberation Now!*, ed. Deborah Babcox and Madeline Belkin (New York: Dell, 1971), pp. 9–24. See also Betty Friedan, *The Feminine Mystique* (New York: Dell, 1963).

2. Harriet Holter, "Sex Roles and Social Change," in *Toward a Sociology of Women*, ed. Constantina Safilios-Rothschild (Lexington, Mass.: Xerox College Publishing, 1972), pp. 331–343.

3. Jeanne Clare Ridley, "The Effects of Population Change on the Roles and Status of Women: Perspective and Speculation," in Safilios-Rothschild, op. cit., pp. 372–386.

4. Holter, op. cit.

5. This discussion is drawn from Jo Freeman, "The Origins of the Women's Liberation Movement," *American Journal of Sociology* 78 (January 1973), pp. 30–49; Judith Hole and Ellen Levine, *Rebirth of Feminism* (New York: Quadrangle Books, 1971); Babcox and Belkin, op. cit.

6. Recently a number of studies have analyzed the social and psychological characteristics of women who join women's liberation groups. Carolyn Stoloff, "Who Joins Women's Liberation?" *Psychiatry* 36 (August 1973), pp. 325–340, found that they were typically middle- or upper-middle-class, urban or suburban, Jewish or Protestant (where religion was not stressed), and much higher than non-members on political activity. Cary Cherniss, "Personality and Ideology: A Personological Study of Women's Liberation," *Psychiatry* 35 (May 1972), pp. 109–125, found women in women's liberation groups were more active and assertive than non-members, and this was accompanied by a sense of strong self-worth and independence. Catherine Arnott, "Feminists and Anti-Feminists as 'True Believers'," *Sociology and Social Research* 57 (April 1973), pp.

300–306, found that rather than women with extreme opposite positions on women's role (NOW and Fascinating Womanhood) sharing the characteristics of "true believers," they were in fact from significantly different sociological pools.

7. Shulamith Firestone, *The Dialectic of Sex* (New York: Bantam, 1970). For other references on the two types of organizational structures, sometimes discussed in terms of three divisions (women's rights, liberation, and socialist), see also Barbara Bovee Polk, "Women's Liberation: Movement for Equality," in Safilios-Rothschild, op. cit., pp. 321–330; Babcox and Belkin, op. cit., introduction; Maren Lockwood Carden, *New Feminist Movement* (New York: Russell Sage, 1974); Hole and Levine, op. cit.; and Freeman, op. cit.

8. See Jessie Bernard, *Women and the Public Interest* (Chicago: Aldine-Atherton, 1971), part V, for further discussion.

9. See, for instance, Babcox and Belkin, introduction, op. cit.; Janet Saltzman Chafetz, *Masculine/Feminine or Human?* (Itasca, Ill.:F. E. Peacock, 1974). Barbara Grizutti Harrison, *Unlearning the Lie: Sexism in School* (New York: Wm. Morrow, 1974). Discussed by Bernard, 1971, op. cit.

10. See Amitai Etzioni, "The Women's Movement—Tokens vs. Objectives," *Saturday Review*, 20 May 1972, p. 34, for a discussion of this issue.

11. Jo Freeman, "The Women's Liberation Movement: Its Origins, Structures, Impact and Ideas," in *Women: A Feminist Perspective*, ed. Jo Freeman (Palo Alto, Calif.: Mayfield, 1975).

12. Ibid., p. 454.

13. Babcox and Belkin, op. cit., p. 4.

14. Margaret Benston, "The Political Economy of Women's Liberation," in Babcox and Belkin, op. cit., pp. 139–144.

15. See, for instance, Marlene Dixon, "Why Women's Liberation?" in Babcox and Belkin, op. cit., pp. 9–24.

16. Friedrich Engels, *The Origin of the Family, Private Property, and the State* (New York: International Publ., 1942).

17. Hole and Levine, op. cit.

18. Sidney Abbott and Barbara Love, *Sappho Was a Right-On Woman, A Liberated View of Lesbianism* (New York: Stein and Day, 1972).

19. Ibid.

20. Radicalesbians, "The Woman-Identified Woman," in Babcox and Belkin, op. cit., pp. 287–293.

21. Harrison, op. cit., p. 75.

22. Ibid.

23. Clarice Stasz Stoll, *Female and Male: Socialization, Social Roles, and Social Structure* (Dubuque, Iowa: Wm. C. Brown, 1974).

24. Freeman, op. cit.

25. These points are suggested by Helen Dudar, "Women's Lib: The War on Sexism," in *The Other Half, Roads to Women's Equality*, ed. Cynthia F. Epstein and Wm. Goode (Englewood Cliffs, N.J.: Spectrum (Prentice-Hall), 1971), pp. 165–176.

26. Posed by Etzioni, op. cit.

27. C. Wright Mills, "Women: The Darling Little Slaves," in *Power, Politics and People*, ed. Irving Louis Horowitz (New York: Ballantine, 1963). The only qualification I would place on his analysis is that women *are* the second sex, and, if they have power, wield it from a position of weakness. This does not make the manipulation any more palatable, however, nor does it imply the need to weigh one kind of oppression against another.

28. Alice S. Rossi, "Sex Equality: The Beginnings of Ideology," in Safilios-Rothschild, op. cit., pp. 344–353.

29. Roxanne Dunbar, "Female Liberation as the Basis for Social Revolution," in *Sisterhood is Powerful*, ed. Robin Morgan (New York: Vintage, 1970), pp. 477–492.

30. Etzioni, op. cit.

31. Institute of Life Insurance, *Public Attitudes Toward the Family, Selected Findings from National Surveys* (New York: Research Services, 1974).

32. Dudar, op. cit.

33. Polk, op. cit.

34. Kirsten Amundsen, *The Silenced Majority, Women and American Democracy* (Englewood Cliffs, N.J.: Prentice-Hall, 1971), p. 168.

35. Kyriakos M. Kontopoulos, "Women's Liberation as a Social Movement," in Safilios-Rothschild, op. cit., pp. 354–361.

36. Chafetz, op. cit.

37. Freeman, op. cit.

38. Glenda Sehested, "A Sociological Examination of the Women's Movement," in *Women and Public Policy: A Humanistic Perspective,* ed. Mildred H. Lavin and Clara H. Oleson (Iowa City: Institute of Public Affairs, Univ. of Iowa, 1974), pp. 135–141.

39. Etzioni, op. cit.

40. For an interesting analysis of the liberation of men, see Warren Farrell, *The Liberated Man* (New York: Random House, 1974).

41. Caroline Bird, *Born Female: The High Cost of Keeping Women Down* (New York: Pocket Books, 1971), p. 215.

42. Freeman, op. cit., p. 460.

43. See Erich Fromm, *Escape from Freedom* (New York: Avon Books, 1941).

ADDITIONAL REFERENCES

1. Chafetz, Janet Saltzman. *Masculine/Feminine or Human?* Itasca, Ill.: F. E. Peacock, 1974.

2. Harrison, Barbara Grizutti. *Unlearning the Lie: Sexism in School.* New York: Wm. Morrow, 1974.

INDEX

AUTHOR INDEX

SUBJECT INDEX

A

Absenteeism, 64, 65
Affirmative action, 78–79
Aging, fear of, 133–35
Alternative (variant) value
    system, 97, 100
Androcentric bias, 35
Androgynous roles, 29
Aristotle, 35, 121

B

Beauty, 132, 136
Bedroom power, 85
Blue-collar marriage, 23–24
Body image, 133
Bona fide occupational
    qualification, 83
Boston Women's Health Book
    Collective, 128

C

Career commitment, 66, 70
Careers, 70
Carmichael, Stokely, 142

Children's textbooks, 37
Christian image of women, 121
Civil Rights Act of 1964, 78, 80,
    83, 142
Colleague family, 16
Common Cause, 80
Communal living, 29
Complementary roles, 15
Consciousness-raising, 144–45
Contingency planning, 67
Counselors, 43
Counterculture marriage, 30
Cult of maternity, 20
Cultural values, 95, 101

D

Dark Lady, 122
Day care, 29
Defensive feminine traits, 23,
    123–24
Democratic ideal (in America), 95
Depression (in women), 130
de Tocqueville, Alexis, 95, 99
Dialectic of Sex, 13
Discrimination on the job (in
    pay), 63, 66, 70
    in employment, 78–79